THE NAMO STORY

OTHER LOTUS TITLES

FORTHCOMING TITLES

THE NAMO STORY

A POLITICAL LIFE

KINGSHUK NAG

LOTUS COLLECTION

ROLI BOOKS

Lotus Collection

© Kingshuk Nag, 2013

This edition published in April 2013
Third impression, November 2013
The Lotus Collection
An imprint of
Roli Books Pvt. Ltd
M-75, Greater Kailash II Market, New Delhi 110 048
Phone: ++91 (011) 4068 2000
Fax: ++91 (011) 2921 7185
E-mail: info@rolibooks.com
Website: www.rolibooks.com
Also at Bengaluru, Chennai, & Mumbai

Editor: Padma Rao Sundarji
Cover design: Bonita Vaz-Shimray
Layout: Sanjeev Mathpal
Production: Shaji Sahadevan
Cover Photograph © Getty Images
Insert: Pages 1, 2-3, 4, 6, 7, 8 © Getty Images
        Page 5 © Press Trust of India

ISBN: 978-81-7436-938-3

Typeset in Adobe Jenson Pro by Roli Books Pvt. Ltd
Printed at Rakmo Press, Okhla, New Delhi.

Contents

Dedicated to the memory of my mother, Manjusri Nag who spent her last days with me in Ahmedabad and passed away in July 2002 as the riots were ebbing.

Author's Note

You can love him, or hate him, depending upon your predilection, but there is no way that you can ignore Narendra Modi. He is one of few, truly enigmatic personalities gracing the contemporary Indian political scene. This is my *raison d'être* for writing his biography. As early as 2004, I could discern that this man would leave behind all his political rivals, including his (then) godfather L.K. Advani, and become the Bharatiya Janata Party's (BJP) official prime ministerial candidate.

In 2009, I was confident that Modi's moment had come, but the opposition within and outside the BJP was so strong that the man had to cap his ambitions for a few more years. In mid-March 2013, as I write this note, there are clear indications of the fact that Modi is racing towards centre stage, aided not only by his resolve but also a weakening Congress regime. His forceful speech, promoting the Gujarat model of development as an alternative to that of the ruling Congress alliance and delivered to the enthralled students of the Delhi University's Shri Ram College of Commerce (SRCC) is a clear indication of his intentions. But the protests that raged outside the college show the opposition that he will have to face on his journey to 7, Race Course Road. They also demonstrated the vastly different reactions that he evokes among the citizens. That this was not an isolated incident is clear from the proposed video talk that Modi was to deliver to students of Wharton in the beginning of March 2013. Even as the talk scheduled was cancelled following protests from a section of the university faculty and student bodies, there was a howl of counter protests. Barely a fortnight before his SRCC speech, Modi offered the services of 'the BJP's Gujarat unit' to the new BJP boss, Rajnath Singh, to strengthen the party nation-wide. Considering that the BJP's Gujarat unit is nothing but Modi (the BJP's Gujarat unit president, an unassuming gentleman lost the 2012 polls as even Modi romped home victorious for the third time), this was a thinly-veiled proposal to be made the prime ministerial candidate for the 2014 general elections. Taking a cue, BJP's senior leader Yashwant Sinha was quick to openly demand that Modi be declared the party's prime ministerial candidate, as his candidature would result in the party getting more votes and seats. Sinha said that during his travels across the country, he had encountered numerous demands from BJP workers and common people that Modi be declared the candidate for the highest executive office. Former actor and now BJP MP, Shatrughan Sinha seconded his proposal even as the new party president, Rajnath Singh, warned party workers against airing their views in public. His contention: it is an intra-party matter and must be decided by BJP's Parliamentary board. Rajnath's warnings (read fears) have fallen on deaf ears as more and more BJP members are joining the Modi bandwagon. Over the next few months, the numbers are bound to swell as the chorus for Modi will reach its crescendo. But let us not harbour any illusions: much of this hype could be the result of a well-orchestrated effort, blessed by none other than Modi himself.

Sinha has vociferously demanded Modi's candidature, but I am not sure how well the two know each other. I have discovered that strangely, most of Modi's fans are not known to him at personal level. Those who do, mistrust his ambition. Modi is highly individualistic and has no friends or family that he is close to. He lives alone and even his mother, who resides with his brother in Gandhinagar, does not come to stay with him. In India, this seems a trifle surprising. But as I said, Modi is unique. Nobody can take him for granted, not even those whom he works with closely. I have seen many politicians of

Modi's own party trying to get his horoscope analyzed by astrologers, in an attempt to figure out what he will do next! The Congress party, clearly on the back foot by the Modi onslaught, is still trying to figure out how to deal with him effectively. The grand old party's responses are mixed and varied. Prime Minister Manmohan Singh, for long the butt of jokes of Modi, reacted by commenting in Parliament that *'jo garajte hai, who baraste nahin'* (those who make tall claims do not deliver). This was in response to Modi's description of the Prime Minister as a 'night watchman' (keeping the wicket safe for Rahul Gandhi). Rahul himself declared Bheeshma like that he would not marry in what was seen as a counter to Modi who never tires of declaring that he does not have a family and thus has no vested interests. However, it seems that like before, the Congress calculates that Modi's controversial image that draws extreme reactions will stymie him. Modi is also aware of this but hopes that if a government delivers good governance and (as he told Indo-Americans in a video address) 'serves the people selflessly then the people will forget the government's mistakes.' This can be read as his fervent prayer that his track of delivering on the economy front will make the voters forget about Godhra.

A book on Modi and Gujarat has been on my mind since the 2002 riots. When I approached a well-known publisher with my book idea, he was candid: 'Write a book from the Hindu point of view and I will publish it'. Disgusted, I shelved the idea. In 2005, I again commenced discussions with a leading publisher, but the project had to be abandoned because this publisher had a diametrically opposite view to the one I held. He felt that a biography of Modi would end up 'lionizing' him.

In July 2012, on a short trip to Delhi, I called on Pramod Kapoor, the publisher of Roli Books and suggested that he allow me to do a biography of Modi that would neither 'demonize' nor 'lionize' the subject. I must thank him and the editorial director of Roli Books, Priya Kapoor, for their faith. Though the information contained in the book was collected over many years, I did not write it at a leisurely pace. From the second week of December 2012 as it became increasingly clear that Modi would sweep the polls once again, the pace had to be quickened. Thanks are therefore due to my editor, Padma Rao Sundarji for coping with the rapid writing towards the end. Neelam Narula also deserves my thanks for fine tuning the copy and ironing out the glitches.

I would also like to thank the management of the *Times of India*, who resisted tremendous pressure to remove me and allowed me to serve in Gujarat in 2002. I am grateful to my colleagues at the *Times of India*, Ahmedabad from whom I have learnt an immense amount. Not to forget my wife Swati, who bore my moods.

Kingshuk Nag
March 2013

Introduction: Winds of Change

When Dr Manmohan Singh, then finance minister of India, initiated the process of economic reforms on 24 July 1991, he had, in all probability, never heard of Narendra Modi. Those days, Modi was trying to make his mark in the Bharatiya Janata Party by organizing various yatras for the likes of L.K. Advani and Murali Manohar Joshi. That sultry afternoon, Singh – who, quoting Victor Hugo, described economic reforms for India as 'an idea whose time had come' – would have been startled if somebody had predicted that the process that he was unleashing would, two decades later, catapult this yatra manager to the gates of Delhi, ready to take on the ruling establishment.

The saga of Narendra Damodardas Modi is the story of how money, religion, beliefs and rising aspirations combined to change the course of Indian politics and economy in the last twenty years. It is also the story of the desire for change among people, albeit without consensus on the nature of change they seek. Above all, it is the saga of economic liberalization unaccompanied by political reforms: a process that led the country from one scam to another.

Sheltered far too long by the license raj, Indian industry, by the end of the 1980s, had become noncompetitive and costly. There was no incentive to reduce costs and no focus on quality. Indian wares were not export-worthy and domestic consumers had no choice. For them, it was a take-it-or-leave-it option. Though exports were not increasing, imports were mounting. This led to a continual mismatch between earnings from exports and the costs of imports. As a result, the country's foreign exchange reserves were depleting. In 1991, reserves fell to a level barely sufficient to finance imports for two weeks. Alarmed, the government pledged gold from RBI's vaults in return for foreign exchange.

In order to extricate the country from this financial mess, P.V. Narasimha Rao, who became prime minister after the 1991 elections, appointed an economist as the finance minister and mandated him to reform the economy.

At the outset, Manmohan Singh devalued the rupee (which made exports cheaper and imports costlier) and removed trade controls. He reasoned that lifting licensing would open Indian industry to competition and compel it to get its act together. As a result, Indian manufacturing would become world class and the consumer would get a huge array of goods hitherto unavailable to him – be it luxury cars, air-conditioners, refrigerators, or washing machines. Above all, this would fuel growth and create employment in a country where the number of unemployed was perpetually rising.

The strategy showed results. Lifting licensing brought in new entrepreneurs in a landscape monopolized by old players whose main strength was to corner licenses, enter into cartel arrangements with co-producers, push shoddy goods into the market, and generally maximize profits. In pursuance of the Say's law of economics that predicts that 'supply creates its own demand' (and not the other way round, as is generally believed), the Indian consumer began to lap up the new products even as the stock markets boomed in an unprecedented bull run. A large part of this bull run was, of course, speculative, but it brought a lot of money into the system. Buoyed by the India growth story and the stories of the 'elephant on the move' and 'the tiger un-caged,' foreign investors with surpluses began arriving in India in droves. For them, India was one of the few countries where the prospects of increased demand remained high: most of the developed world had saturated markets.

Doing away with industrial licenses had another effect: the scene shifted to states. Previously, it was the business of the Government of India to decide who could manufacture what, and in what quantities. Now, the winds of change had begun to blow. Entrepreneurs could decide what they wanted to manufacture, and more importantly, where. The last was crucial because it drove competition between states to attract investments to their territories. Businessmen were in raptures because they could now command chief ministers and demand the goodies they wanted as incentives to set up plants in their states. At the same time, chief ministers became more important: an enterprising chief minister dealing directly with businesses could create an entirely different political constituency.

An ancient saying in north India lists 'zar, zoroo aur zameen' (money, woman and land) – though not in the order of importance – as the main causes for human disputes. True or not, the saying reflects the feudal mores prevailing in the country for centuries. Even a few years of liberalization could not change this mindset: businessmen began to clamour increasingly for cheap land in return for investing their money in a given state.

Simultaneously, something else happened. Though reforms were aimed at making Indian industry and manufacturing internationally competitive, entrepreneurs showed more interest in the services sector. This was not surprising considering India's large labour pool. Most of the labour force was young, underutilized and raring to go. More importantly it came cheap and was, by and large, proficient in English. Entrepreneurs realized that this strength of India could be harnessed. Be it information technology (IT), software programming, financial accounting, or information technology-enabled services like call centres or Y2K and medical transcription, India was on the way to becoming the back office of the world. But whether genetic or not, even those Indian entrepreneurs who set up technology companies could not shed this desire to own cheap land.

Jobs in these growing services sectors rapidly led to increased aspirations. Employees began to aspire towards better lifestyles and own their own homes. If their fathers had built their nesting places just before retirement with all the money accumulated in provident funds, the 25+ generation wanted to own property by age 30.

Sensing an opportunity, many entrepreneurs rushed into the realty sector. Many companies set up real estate divisions and mixed the profits from realty with those from their other businesses. By doing this, they lent the illusion of higher profits, which would, in turn, translate into more attractive scrip prices on the bourses. In this way, more funds could be accessed from the market. A good example of such a phenomenon was the scam-struck Satyam Computers whose promoter Ramalinga Raju's considerable side business – if not his main business – was land purchase and trade.

Realty requires funds, but not as much as manufacturing does. More important for the realty business is access to cheap land. In an expanding urban scenario, this can only be had from farm lands in villages on the periphery of the city. But accessing such land requires rules to be relaxed to allow conversion of the land to non-agricultural use. A few years into the reforms process, businesses began seeking land liberalization laws with permission for corporate investment in land. Soon, new concepts like special economic zones (SEZs) were floated. Through SEZs, corporations wanted control over all land surrounding their business zones for housing, fun, and recreation. Some of them wanted to control the sea front and sought vast tracts of land next to ports they wanted to build. All this was sought in the name of making manufacturing world-class. For instance, they argued that townships near factories could facilitate – and motivate – the work force. But to the shrewd, it was clear that all this was nothing but a desire to own real estate.

Though liberalization was expected to usher in changes in the economy in its wake, nobody had reckoned that it would transform the practice of politics in the country. But this is exactly what happened.

With huge profits to be made from realty, an increasing number of politicians began to enter the business, a trend which worked in the reverse too. The nexus between politics and business grew closer. If it was taboo for politicians to be associated with business in the good old days, this was now no longer the case.

At the same time, politics too, was getting costlier: something waiting to happen, because nobody had thought of reforming the political system along with economic reforms. A rise in regional aspirations and heightened caste consciousness since Independence impacted the polity and made it intensely competitive. At the same time the opportunities for public offices remained limited. The population of the country was increasing significantly but the number of legislative assembly and Lok Sabha seats remained fixed. Though the number of people aspiring to run for elections was increasing, the number of seats was not. This was due to a strange reason: in 1971 it was found that although the population of the country was growing, it was not increasing uniformly across states. This meant that if the number of seats in the Lok Sabha would have to be increased to reflect this population growth, the states where population grew faster would corner more seats. This would lead to a rebalancing of political power between states and those states where population grew the slowest would suffer more. To prevent this, a law was passed in the mid-'70s freezing the number of Lok Sabha and legislative assembly seats till 2001. However in 2001, this freeze was extended till 2031. This freeze had the effect of making politics expensive. Firstly, the number of voters in each seat increased: so candidates had to reach a larger number and this meant more money spent. With more candidates for each seat, more money was spent. In fact, running for public offices became so costly that only those with deep pockets could hope to succeed. There was no place in this system for honest, hard-working candidates with no motives other than the good of society.

In all probability, Narendra Modi had little clue of how things would pan out when he was organizing the numerous yatras in the early 1990s. His worldview had been defined by the Rashtriya Swayamsevak Sangh (RSS), an organization that he sought refuge in when he came to Ahmedabad, after leaving his home and hearth in Vadnagar in 1967. The circumstances which prompted the young Narendra to leave home are not absolutely clear. However, the 'search for an identity' surely played a role in this decision. The RSS, perpetually on the hunt for young blood, roped in Modi and this was one of the biggest factors to shape his life. Founded in 1925, RSS is seen as a right-wing Hindu force. Though *Vasudhaiva Kutumbakum* – the whole universe is a family – is the motto of the organization, the general belief is that its thinly-disguised agenda is to establish a country based on Hindu nationalism. Other religions also have a role in the RSS worldview, but they are secondary. In any case, proponents of all religions in the country have been influenced by the Hindu way of life. This is the philosophy that Modi came to be influenced by, in the course of the next two decades, even as he became a full-time pracharak of the RSS, working from the Hegdewar Bhavan office in Ahmedabad.

The RSS is not a single organization: it has a parivar of smaller outfits around the mothership. All the outfits are structured to further the objectives of the RSS. Some of them work for the benefit of students, others for women and yet others for tribals. To ensure that the RSS's philosophy is not diluted, representatives from the RSS are embedded in these organizations and they guide the core activities. A political party is an essential component of the RSS family. After Independence, it was the Jana Sangh that the RSS used to operate through. The Jana Sangh, however, had limited influence on people and was localized to a few north Indian states. The Emergency imposed by Indira Gandhi lasted merely 19 months, but it brought about momentous changes in politics in India. For the first time, the Opposition tried to unite upon a common platform. Thus, the Janata Party was formed. The party, however, broke up a few years later precisely over the demand by some members of the erstwhile Jana Sangh for dual membership. They wanted to be part of the Janata Party and also the RSS. Others in the Janata Party found this galling and soon the party collapsed. The Jana Sangh was back in a new avatar: the Bharatiya Janata Party. The new name was to project a new brand image for the party that had earlier been restricted by its image of being a strong Hindu force.

But the BJP, being restricted to two Lok Sabha seats, failed to make any significant headway in the 1984 year-end elections. It was at this time that the party with a new helmsman – L.K. Advani – decided to go back to its old agenda, but with new symbolism.

The new symbol was the Ram Janmabhoomi and the objective: a temple for Lord Rama at the spot where he was supposedly born. This was in Ayodhya, at the site of a masjid constructed by generals of the first Mughal emperor Babar. The BJP would have to be geared up for this purpose: this meant a pan-Hindu mobilization across the nation, culminating at the site in Ayodhya. Advani went about the task energetically, infusing new blood into the party from within the Sangh parivar. In Gujarat, one of his chosen men was Narendra Modi. Now thirty-seven years of age, Modi's induction into the BJP in 1987 was the second biggest event in his life.

Notwithstanding the paeans sung to Indian democracy, politics, in this country, is much about caste and communities. Caste often determines the interests of Indian political organizations, including those of mainstream parties. If a particular dominant caste group is aligned with a party, its competitors in the rural economy will invariably join the rival formation. This is true all across India. In Gujarat, the Congress party reflected the interests of the Patels, till a strong OBC movement was launched within the party by a combination of the Pradesh Congress chief Jinabhai Darji and Madhavsinh Solanki, the new chief minister, in the early 1980s. This made the Patels (the upwardly-mobile caste of the 1980s and beneficiaries of land reforms and a green revolution) launch a search for a new alternative. Those were early days for the BJP, and it was a party in search of a core support group. The only supporters of the party were those who were adherents of the RSS. But the problem is that RSS did not represent any caste group in the countryside: where the majority of the population lived. So there were the Patels, a caste group in search of a party, and the BJP, which was a party in search of adherents. The fit was perfect. Increasingly, behind its veneer of Hindutva and the Ram temple movement at national level, the party began reflecting the interests of the Patels.

Around 1995 when the BJP came to power on the shoulders of the Patels in Gujarat, liberalization was already four years old. Liberalization suited the Patels well: they lapped up its benefits. With increased farm productivity, their incomes had grown drastically. They now wanted to spend money on more goods. They also wanted to invest more: in gold, stocks, and land. The last was only natural, considering that for many hundred of years their livelihoods had been drawn from land. Many of them now started migrating to the cities getting into realty, trade, and other kinds of businesses. In power, the BJP was to unabashedly become a Patel party, changing and amending policies as would suit its needs. If land reforms were the leitmotif of the government in earlier decades, it was land liberalization that now formed the cornerstone of policy. This was a bit ironical: in the '50s the Patels, tillers of land till then, had gained ownership of land, courtesy redistribution policies that were inspired by socialist visions and brought in by governments of the day. But now, they wanted land to be a tradable commodity. Bowing to Patel pressure, the BJP government led by Keshubhai Patel, eased laws relating to land trade. Previously, farm land could be bought only by farmers who lived within a radius of 8 kilometre from the land. Now, anybody could buy land.

The BJP government was following a dual policy: on the one hand, it was pursuing matters that addressed the business interests of the Patels, and indeed, those of the new urban community including upwardly-mobile groups whose economic ambitions closely resembled those of the Patels.

On the other, the BJP was forced to support the Hindutva agenda of the affiliates of the Sangh parivar who were becoming increasingly active in the state where their own party ruled. The common public did not perceive any dichotomy in this. Fed on novels that fictionalized history and painted in gory colours the iconoclastic nature of invaders like Mahmud of Ghazni, society was becoming polarized (such novels had been popular since the beginning of the twentieth century). Increased mobilization by Sangh parivar affiliates was only strengthening this world view. I was witness to this when I first went to live in Gujarat in 2000. When I called on Keshubhai Patel, the first sentence that the chief minister uttered was: '*badal dalo, badal dalo,* pro-Christian stand *badal dalo.*' He was referring to the anti-Christian riots in Dang district of Gujarat where the TOI reportage had been openly critical of his government. When I looked askance, Keshubhai said: '*Main nahin kahta, log kahte hain.*' Thus, the BJP government was simultaneously pursuing policies of liberalization and Hindutva when Narendra Modi came to the helm in October 2001.

Famous medieval historian, Percival Spear, identified four factors that affected the stability of the Mughal Empire. One was the balance of the internal power structure, the second, relations with powers with whom it shared borders. The third was the personality and strength of the emperor, and the fourth, the robustness of the economy. Analyzing Modi's raj along these lines, his initial months were troublesome. Nobody expected him to last. But after the Gujarat riots of 2002, the state began to rally behind him. This was natural: polarization, set in motion by the advent of the BJP government in 1995, was now complete. Adivasis in tribal Gujarat – though never Hindus – began to see themselves as the progeny of those who believed in the faith of Lord Rama. Dalits, who were antagonistic towards upper classes, were getting subsumed into this larger Hindu identity. In a bid for rapid consolidation, the Sangh parivar affiliates – whether by design or otherwise – had used the 'we and others' theory. The 'we' were the Hindus. The 'others' were the Muslims who had made their appearance in the then largely Hindu country through conquests in medieval times. With the rulers being Muslims, many of their Hindu subjects converted, either because they were forced to do so or because the economic benefits of conversion were huge. Now, the 'others' were being seen as obstructionists in the Hindu cause. The Godhra train incident coalesced about 50 per cent of the Gujarati Hindus in a common identity like never before, as they rallied behind Modi. This expanded the Patel support base of the party. Patels, by themselves, accounted for not more than 20 per cent of the population of the state.

Spear's observation about the Mughal relationship with external powers can be compared with Modi's relations with the central government. In 2002, a government headed by his own party was in power in Delhi. Half the population of Gujarat had rallied behind him. Nationally, there was widespread condemnation of Gujarat in 2002. And yet, the BJP could not remove one of its own men from power as he had, after all, consolidated 'Hindutva'. This insulated Modi from trouble and although there were efforts to dislodge him, the party hawks managed a counter coup and kept Modi intact. Some of them were to privately lament this in the future, when Modi became more powerful, invincible and increasingly began to call the shots. Simultaneously, though he had total control in Gujarat, he reduced the Sangh parivar and the BJP to ciphers. Modi went into elections in 2012 asking voters to not look at individual candidates, but to vote for him. 'Don't look at the candidates, assume that you are voting for me directly,' he exhorted. If insiders are to be believed, many top RSS functionaries in Gujarat would have loved for Modi to lose the last elections.

Gujarat's economy had always been robust, and its people industrious and enterprising. The road to a modern Gujarat began to be laid in the 1970s, but an aggressive push was given in the early 1990s by Chief Minister Chimanbhai Patel in his second term, just as the economic reforms were taking shape. Being on the west coast had its own advantages and Reliance gave a major thrust by building a huge petroleum refinery with a capacity of 27 million metric tons per annum, expanding it to a 62 million tons per annum over the years. Essar also decided on its 11 million ton per annum capacity refinery close by and set-up a big steel plant in Hazira, close to Surat in south Gujarat. The Adanis, too, set up a private port in Mudhra, in Kutch, before the 2001 earthquake. Most of their investments began fructifying before Narendra Modi took over as the chief minister. The growth in the economy was also due to harnessing the waters of the Narmada, much of which was wasted as it flowed into the Arabian Sea. The impounding of the waters (through a multipurpose dam) was not without a hitch. Activists like Medha Patkar swung into action. The project was commenced during the time of Chimanbhai but the benefits started accruing during the regime of Keshubhai and more in the times of Modi.

It is to the credit of Modi that he was able to build on the growth momentum imparted by Chimanbhai. Aiding him in this, of course, was the process of economic reforms at the national level which had expanded and deepened growth. All states – whether Maharashtra and Karnataka or laggards like Bihar and Rajasthan – were growing faster than before. In the previous years, Gujarat has grown at an average of 10 per cent per annum. This is significantly higher than the 6.5 per cent per annum recorded in the earlier decade. The levels of poverty fell: from 31.6 per cent in 2004-05 to 23 per cent in 2009-10. This was a good performance, but obviously a lot more needed to be done. Simultaneously, many Congress-ruled states started conjuring up welfare measures, ostensibly to boost the condition of the poor, but actually to secure a vote bank. The best example of this was seen in Andhra Pradesh, where Chief Minister Y.S. Rajasekhara Reddy began a regime of seven hours of free power to farmers, medical insurance to the poor even for surgical interventions, reimbursement of college fees to backward students, and other measures. The state's coffers would have been depleted, were it not for the fact that the government became a realtor and raised up to ₹1200 crore from auctioning government-owned land. Such 'freebies' were to distort state economies but they shored up the political prospects of the Congress.

Modi, to his credit, never took recourse to such populist moves, although with 50 per cent of the Gujarati Hindus behind him, there was no compelling reason to do so. The net result of this, however, is that Gujarat is a revenue surplus state with the base of the economy not eroded by a culture of handouts. The state, located in the western part of India and far from India's domestic coal mines, had for long seen a costly power regime. This had hampered the process of electrification in rural Gujarat. Modi, who as a boy in a small town had experienced days and nights without electricity, decided on a novel 'Jyotigram village scheme' to provide electricity to the state's 18,065 villages by 2003. The villages were to have assured power supply but they would have to pay for it. Even Modi's critics concede that the project was a success. In the olden days, this privilege had been restricted to a few affluent households in the villages.

Though the power has to be paid for and losses from Transmission and Distribution (T&D) are high, the situation is still better than in Andhra Pradesh, where free power costs the exchequer over ₹1200 crore annually. Though the social indicators of Gujarat are poor, it is the strong and grounded economy, guided by Modi's common sense and practicality, that has shored up the state.

In the present day scenario, Gujarat's fortunes are influenced most of all by the strength and personality of Modi. Though Modi is described as a brilliant administrator, his strength lies in tapping into and getting in synch with the public mood. By linking his fortunes with those of his people, Modi is much more than a mere arbiter of their destinies. This was most evident in the case of the 2002 Gujarat riots. Though he should have tried hard to quell the riots, perhaps

Modi may have believed that trying to do so would result in his getting upstaged. So, instead of trying to control the riots, he stood by as a passive spectator. His critics, however, allege that he was more than just that.

An interesting tale did the rounds in Gujarat in 2002: VHP secretary, Praveen Togadia, was annoyed with Modi and asked him why he was getting the credit, when it was Togadia's men who had been active. There is no way to check the authenticity of the story but after the riots, Modi was indeed able to establish himself as the Hindu *hriday samrat*, the guy who could be banked on to take the Hindus to greater glory, while, Togadia by comparison, paled into – relative – insignificance. The new labeling of Modi established him head and shoulders above both his seniors and contemporaries in Gujarat politics. But it was precisely the riots that made him unacceptable to the rest of India. Modi's challenge was how to surmount this obstacle. Cultivating other powerful constituencies came in handy. As noted earlier, reforms brought a new spring to the step of businessmen constantly in search of benefits. Modi realized that building the image of a Mandrake who could conjure up all that entrepreneurs wanted, was a good way to ensure success. His 'Vibrant Gujarat' shows helped him in this endeavour. Quick clearances and elimination of red tape were essential parts of this exercise. Businessmen had never seen anybody like him before (except for Chandrababu Naidu for a brief while in Andhra Pradesh) and were ecstatic. Businesses came from far and wide: from all parts of the country and the world, and sought his benefaction. They still do. During that process, Modi lost his support base among others. But the loss was not enough to negate his other gains. Ask the residents of Sanand, part of Greater Ahmedabad where Ratan Tata set up his shining Nano factory with the help of a hitherto unseen quantum of goodies (Modi also paid for the transportation of the half-built Nano plant from Singur in West Bengal to Gujarat). The irony is that the electors of Sanand have voted out Modi's *manas* and have elected a Congress candidate from the seat. Local caste factors are held responsible for this.

Myth-building is an important weapon in Modi's armoury, while the cultivation of the image of a *vikas purush* (a development man) has allowed him to counter alternative world views. A few years ago when the powerful local business group Nirma, run by Karsanbhai Patel, decided to set up a cement plant in Bhavanagar district of coastal Gujarat, few believed that the project would be stymied. That it then happened due to the efforts of a BJP MLA in Modi's Gujarat seemed unbelievable. Nirma wanted land right in the middle of a water body on the coast and private agricultural land amounting to 4415 acres. The lease of the land would affect nine villages: in fact it would completely annihilate seven of them. Three-time local BJP MLA, Kanu Kalsaria, revolted and appealed to Modi but to no avail. Kalsaria then launched his own Sadbhavana front and moved the Supreme Court. The apex court cancelled the project. The interesting thing to note is that neither Modi nor the BJP took any action against Kalsaria even when the latter, all fire and brimstone, accused Modi of *show baazi*. 'His Sadbhavana is nothing but show business for publicity and spoils that do not translate into the greater good', fumed Kalsaria. The MLA later quit the BJP and stood for elections on his own. When he lost the 2012 elections, it was proof that although he had local support (on the basis of which he had organized the Sadbhavana front), the voter was ready to go with Modi and his image of being a development man.

A lot of myths around Modi and his economic prowess are based on half-truths and gross exaggerations. Modi's well-publicized Vibrant Gujarat shows convey the impression that Gujarat leads other states in attracting foreign investment. But, the truth is that Gujarat has received only 5 per cent of foreign investments in India in the last twelve years. Maharashtra and the National Capital Region of Delhi are far ahead.

Nowadays and more often than not, the website of the Gujarat State Petroleum Corporation (GSPC) does not open easily.

It is as though the heads of GSPC do not want information about the company to go public. But this was not always the case. On a Sunday at the end of June 2005 and during torrential monsoon rain over the city of Ahmedabad, Narendra Modi suddenly called for an evening press conference. Jolted out of their post-lunch stupor, media persons tore to the Sardar Patel Institute of Public Administration to figure out what the matter was. Modi was at his ebullient best: 'I am proud to announce the biggest gas find in India. We have discovered more than 20 trillion cubic feet (tcf) of gas. GSPC has discovered this gas which is valued upwards of $50 billion,' Modi said. The gas had been struck at the distant Krishna Godavari Basin off the coast of Andhra Pradesh, where GSPC had taken up exploration. Modi's officials were quick to point out that the discovery made by GSPC was higher than the 14 trillion cubic feet (tcf) discovered by Reliance Industries Limited (RIL) in the same basin.

The excitement generated by the GSPC announcement soon prompted Modi to urge the state government-owned company to go international. GSPC took up blocks in Egypt, Australia, Yemen, and Indonesia. Earlier, Modi had signed an MoU with Russia's Astrakhan province for the same purpose.

But less than eight years later, the GSPC bubble burst. After some false indicators, the discovery proved to be nothing but a mirage. The Directorate-General of Hydrocarbons, which independently evaluates such 'discoveries', had figured out that the find was not worth 20 tcf but only about 2 tcf. GSPC managers realized that even 2 tcf would be difficult to extract because the costs would be very high. According to a senior official of the GSPC, Modi was informed about all this two years ahead. He heard the matter out and said nothing more. Obviously, no public announcements were made, but GSPC had, reputedly, borrowed upwards of ₹9000 crore to fund the exploration that has, so far, yielded little. While campaigning for Election 2012, Arvind Kejriwal, too, had brandished documents to show that GSPC had entered into a partnership with a company based in Barbados and thrown away its stakes for a pittance. This, apparently, rattled Modi who had built his image on probity.

Modi may not have berated his officials. But subsequently, and in a bid to cover up all this and be seen as a successful venture, GSPC has spawned several subsidiaries in related businesses like gas transmission, gas purchase, and sale and even supply of gas to domestic households.

In the first week of October 2012, GSPC bought 65 per cent equity in Gujarat Gas Company, an entity owned, till then, by British Gas, an MNC. If newspaper reports are to be believed, there was an element of coercion in the takeover. By raising the prices of supplies, Gujarat Gas, which supplies domestic gas in Ahmedabad, was locked in a dispute with the Gujarat government.

Later, British Gas put up Gujarat Gas for sale. Media reports allege that Adani Gas and Torrent Power, two private companies interested in the purchase, were advised to keep away. In the end, GSPC took over Gujarat Gas at a cost of ₹2694 crore: a heavy discount from the market price of ₹4000 crore that British Gas was expecting. Barely three weeks later, on 21 October, Britain's High Commissioner in India, John Bevan, called on Modi, ending ten years of boycott of the Gujarat chief minister. Her Majesty's government announced that the engagement was to further British business interests in Gujarat. Thus, Modi was able to achieve two objectives: provide for a profitable revenue stream for the down-in-the-dumps GSPC, and rein in the British, whose attitude had been troubling him for long.

Narendra Modi is what he is, also because some others are not what they should have been. This point was made tellingly by K.P.S. Gill (who had been posted as security advisor to Modi in May 2002 when the riots showed no signs of petering out) in a private meeting with representatives of civil society. He said: 'The Government of Gujarat would have been forced to act had Sonia Gandhi air-dashed to Gandhinagar on 28 February and sat on a dharna outside the Raj Bhavan. There is no way that action would not have been taken,' he declared. Sonia was, at the time, leader of the Opposition and her Congressmen in Gujarat were nowhere to be seen in public, while the riots raged in the state. It was obvious that the Congress lacked the strength of ideological conviction to counter Modi.

Nawal Kishore Sharma was appointed governor of Gujarat in July 2004, soon after the UPA came into power. Sharma, a dyed-in-the-wool Congressman, had been dispatched to keep an eye on the state of affairs under Modi. In my first meeting with him, before I could even sit down, the governor said: 'Whatever you say, you have to give credit to the devil.' Sharma held this opinion even though it was still early days, and much of Modi's prowess in formulation and execution of economic policies was yet to unfold.

Conversations with Shankersinh Vaghela, who was inducted into the Manmohan Singh cabinet at that time, too reflected the 'dual' policy of the Congress. Vaghela lamented many times to me that important party men in Delhi were against taking on Modi because they felt it would aggravate the situation for the Congress. Vaghela himself, a former RSS man who had seen Modi from close quarters, thought otherwise. 'He is a bully who has to be taken by the horns,' Vaghela told me many times. Civil society activists like Shabnam Hashmi and Teesta Setalvad, who have worked for long in Gujarat, also lament this lack of conviction on part of the Congress to take on Modi. 'Sometimes, it seems that some Congressmen are closet admirers of Modi,' Hashmi says.

Part of the popularity of Modi outside Gujarat has been due to the increasing incidence of mega-scams in recent years and a perceived crisis of leadership. Since Modi has a clean image as far as governance is concerned, these scandals and perceptions serve to contrast the Gujarat chief minister against the existing, dismal state of affairs. As somebody remarked: people are fed up with the breakdown around them. They are looking for a strong leader who, they think, can deliver. Modi's name is being conjured up in the context, although it is a matter of great doubt whether the Gujarat strong man (especially with his communal record) can live up to this expectation. That is, if given a chance.

I

Can he become Prime Minister?

It takes neither a degree in rocket science, nor one in psephology, to guess who was happiest when Narendra Modi won the Gujarat assembly elections for the third time in a row. Of course, the party in question will never admit to its euphoria in public. But when Modi took oath at a glittering event at Ahmedabad's Sardar Patel Stadium, leaders of the Congress – albeit privately – applauded the loudest. To them, Modi's latest victory was a certain sign that the Gujarat chief minister will invariably make his way towards Delhi as the BJP's next prime ministerial candidate in 2014 – and therewith consolidate minority votes across the nation against the BJP and in favour of the Congress.

'Muslims in Gujarat – to some extent – may have made their peace with Modi, but in minority circles across the nation, he is nothing but a hate figure. His projection of being a great performer on the economic front cuts no ice with the minorities,' says a senior Congress leader.

India's electoral system – called the first-past-the-post (FPTP) and borrowed from Great Britain – does not require a candidate (or a party) to get a majority of votes to be elected. Often candidates and parties come to power based on minority votes. A striking illustration of this is the vote share of the Congress party in the 2004 and 2009 elections: 26.53 per cent and 28.55 per cent respectively. In fact, political analysts say that in elections contested by multiple parties, a government can easily come to power with a mere 30 per cent of all votes cast. This works out to an even smaller percentage of the total number of voters, considering that a significant portion of the electorate does not exercise its right to franchise.

Now weigh the fact that Muslims make up nearly 15 per cent of the electorate (as per the latest estimates). With Modi being projected as the BJP's prime ministerial candidate, Congress circles believe that Muslims will vote for the Congress with a vengeance. To get another 15 per cent is not that difficult a proposition and garnering a total of 30 per cent is not such a great deal, feel Congress leaders. In fact, the victory of the Congress-led alliance in both 2004 and 2009, is attributed to the votes that it got from Muslims. This was topped up by votes from other sections. The performance of the Vajpayee government (1999-2004) was good and India was really 'shining'. In 2004, liberalization – initiated in 1991 – was more than a decade old and the benefits of reforms were being felt across India in the form of higher disposable incomes and better lifestyles. Vajpayee's image was good and the government did not provoke a strong anti-incumbency. Yet, much to the surprise of analysts, the BJP-led NDA government was booted out of power. What happened?

'Vajpayee had made an attempt to make Modi quit his post in 2002, but failed. The consolidation of Hindu votes in Gujarat brought Modi back to power in Gujarat, but the consolidation of minority votes against the BJP, forced the government out of power in New Delhi,' confesses a BJP insider. The same sentiment returned the Congress-led alliance to power in 2009, at a time when there were murmurs that Modi could possibly cross over to Delhi. 'The Congress allowed itself to be destroyed in Gujarat by Modi, but in the process strengthened itself at the federal level,' chuckles a Congress leader.

The Congress is hoping for an encore in 2014, but politics seldom follows a predictable path. For one, Muslims are fed up of being taken for granted by the Congress government. They feel that they have nowhere else to go and that with the BJP around, they will have no option but to vote for the Congress. But this is a fallacious belief,' says Altaf Hussain, a Muslim businessman from Mumbai. 'I would say that many Congress leaders are soft Hindutva proponents who pay only lip service to our cause.'

Changing alignments in the Muslim pattern of voting have been confirmed by the estrangement of the Majlis-Ittehadul-Muslimeen (MIM) from the Congress. Staunch allies for nearly three decades, the MIM, which is a force in Hyderabad (where Muslims constitute some 35 per cent of the population) has walked out of the UPA alliance in New Delhi and the Congress government in Andhra Pradesh. Though he refrains from calling Sonia Gandhi names, MIM party chief, Assaduddin Owaisi, has been shouting from the rooftops that the Andhra Pradesh chief minister is 'communal'. MIM is now expected to join hands with a breakaway Congress faction: the YSR Congress led by Jagan Reddy. The latter, who has ruled out a tie-up with the BJP, favours a loose alliance of third parties across the nation. Such an alliance may potentially include the Nationalist Congress Party (NCP) of Sharad Pawar in Maharashtra and Mulayam Singh Yadav's Samajwadi Party in UP. This alliance may tilt the Muslim votes in its favour, so the Congress gambit may be misplaced. But this will be of little solace to Narendra Modi, other than the fact that the two combinations may undercut each other. In fact, this is what has happened in the recent Gujarat elections over some seats: though the Congress could have won because of sizeable Muslim votes, the BJP did. The presence of Muslim independent candidates divided the vote, thereby affecting the Congress. A prime example was the Jamalpur-Khadia assembly seat in Ahmedabad, where Muslims account for 60 per cent of the votes. Yet the BJP had the last laugh, because up against the Congress Muslim candidate, was another – rebel Congress Muslim. They cut into each others' votes and – the BJP candidate sailed through.

Senior leaders of BJP are falling over each other to congratulate Modi and hail him as the suitable prime ministerial candidate. Many of them, both BJP national leaders as well as satraps of different states scrambled to Ahmedabad to attend Modi's investiture. Still, insiders say that they would not want him to leave the party. 'Even the RSS, the mother organization of the Sangh parivar where Modi began his political life, is opposed to him,' claims a party insider. 'The RSS is a disciplined party but everybody who knows him well is aware that Modi will not listen to Nagpur at all and hijack the BJP to serve his own end,' the insider, who has risen from the ranks of the RSS and is now in the BJP, discloses. Incidentally, the RSS even in Gujarat is opposed to Modi because of his 'self-willed' ways. If party veterans are to be believed, the trio of L.K. Advani, Arun Jaitely, and Sushma Swaraj, too, would like to keep Modi at bay. 'Advani is already eighty-five years old. This is his last chance to become prime minister. He would not like Modi to upstage him,' party sources reveal. Though Advani was Modi's original benefactor in the BJP, those who keep close tabs on the relations between the two, aver that the former is totally dependent on the Gujarat chief minister to get elected to the Lok Sabha from the Gandhinagar constituency. They also point to how Modi drew more applause at election rallies they have jointly addressed since 2004.

The crafty 'legal eagle', Arun Jaitely, is close to Modi and has contributed hugely to the latter's cause. 'Jaitely is a great strategist and a brilliant lawyer. But he has no political base of his own,' says the insider. He deduces that even if a BJP-led coalition comes close to power, it could succeed only if it has a prime ministerial candidate acceptable to all. 'That means a Manmohan Singh-type of prime minister. Jaitely feels that he himself could fit the bill,' a party insider asserts. Of course, there is no concrete proof of Jaitely's strategy. But the source says that if Modi fails to become prime minister himself, Jaitely wants Modi should support him. The argument is that since the lawyer has no political base, Modi will not be threatened by him, and therefore he can afford to bide his time as Jaitely holds the reins. But in the corridors of power in Delhi, the belief is that the relations between Modi and Jaitely have been a bit frosty off late. This would imply that if push comes to shove, it cannot be taken for granted that Modi will root for Jaitely who is a Rajya Sabha MP from Gujarat and has got a fresh, six-year mandate in 2010. But the days preceding his nomination were marked by intense speculation that the Delhi lawyer would have to seek accommodation from some other state.

Sushma Swaraj reportedly nurtures the ambition to be the first woman prime minister of the BJP. Indeed, during Shiv Sena supremo Bal Thackeray's lifetime, she had sought and secured his support too. But to the RSS, Swaraj is suspect because of her husband Swaraj Kaushal's socialist background. There is no love lost between her and Modi either. Her comments at Vadodara amidst the heat of electioneering, that Modi could be a prime ministerial candidate, is attributed to convoluted political logic that only politicians can make head or tail of. In the words of a BJP insider, Sushma, by projecting Modi as a prime ministerial candidate, wanted to keep him in Gujarat till 2014 and prevent him from becoming the BJP president. The argument goes that as BJP president in Delhi, Modi would consolidate his position faster than if he were to remain in Gandhinagar as the chief minister. In the event Modi did not press for his candidature after Nitin Gadkari stepped down. This was perhaps due to strategic reasons and internal opposition.

Strong BJP chief ministers like Shivraj Singh Chauhan of Madhya Pradesh and Raman Singh of Chattisgarh have not shown any inclination to bid for the top post. But the possibility of throwing in their hats at a later stage cannot be discounted. 'Our chief minister's performance has been brilliant. Chauhan is a great administrator and has brought so much investment into the state. But he works silently and does not make a big song and dance like Modi. He is good material to be a prime minister,' says Anil Sharma, a merchant from Indore and a BJP supporter. There is similar support for Raman Singh whose firm stand against Maoists is cited as evidence of his being a strong man.

It is not that Modi does not know of these inner machinations of senior leaders of his party. But he also knows that he is very popular with the middle-rung leaders and the rank-and-file of the party, the kinds of people whose personal ambitions don't clash with his and who are looking for a leader who can take them to victory. Modi knows that it is only a BJP victory that can give such smaller leaders a share of the spoils of office. He is also aware that these leaders consider him the only one cut out for the job. 'Modi sahib will overpower the opposition inside the party because of the massive support he enjoys at the grass-roots level. The BJP bosses may lock the doors in Delhi, but our leader will break open the lock and with the tremendous support of the state party workers he will be anointed as the BJP's PM candidate. A chief minister like Shivraj Singh Chauhan can be good but they cannot lead the party to victory nationally,' says a Modi acolyte in Gujarat.

Most analysts in New Delhi agree that Modi will move to Delhi sometime in 2013, or influence the composition of BJP office bearers in such a way that those with personal allegiance to him will be in the majority. Elections are slated in Chattisgarh and Madhya Pradesh at the end of 2013. Both the BJP chief ministers there are doing well. Modi will try to take credit for their victories by positioning himself in Delhi or having his men run the national affairs of the party. If BJP had won in Himachal Pradesh too, Modi, by virtue of having been the BJP secretary for HP many years ago, would have most certainly taken credit for it.

'In some ways you don't have to formally designate him as prime ministerial candidate of the BJP, he is already so in public perception,' a political analyst suggests.

Though it is virtually a fait accompli that Modi will be the BJP's prime ministerial candidate, can he actually pull off a victory and occupy South Block? Or will the Congress gambit pay off? Analysts say that if minority votes consolidate against Modi, Hindu votes can similarly consolidate in his favour as a reaction. In the past two elections, minority votes have silently consolidated in favour of the Congress and against the BJP, without anyone even realizing it. This time, the hope for such a consolidation happening silently is near zero. On the other hand, there is bound to be a counter-consolidation of Hindu votes. But how strong this sentiment will be cannot be easily predicted. The most notable example of consolidation of Hindu votes is that which happened when the Ram Janmabhoomi movement was on. Unlike the one-shot affair that voting for a Modi-led BJP would be, that consolidation happened over several years. Then at the height of the movement, BJP did not get more than 120 seats in 1991 and 85 seats in 1989. In sharp contrast, the party got many more seats in 1996, 1998 and 1999 when it did not take recourse to the Hindu agenda. Political analysts like Hindutva expert Jyotirmaya Sharma say that in reality there is nothing as the Hindu vote, which is why the BJP gave it up. However, they feel that Modi, with his penchant for jingoism, can raise the pitch by targeting Pakistan and infiltrators from Bangladesh. Confined to Gujarat till now, Modi has not taken much interest in commenting about affairs pertaining to Bangladesh. But now, this could change and Modi could well rabble-rouse about the demographic profile of Assam and West Bengal getting altered by continual infiltration from Bangladesh. This might lead to a polarization of the so-called Hindu vote, but nobody can yet predict to what extent. This jingoism has takers in communities across India, which is why many jetsetters, whether in Mumbai, Delhi or Bengaluru, find the prospects of his elevation to prime minister attractive. 'He is popular even in places like Kerala and West Bengal,' says a police officer.

There is another, potentially insurmountable road block in Modi's way: even if the BJP acquiesces to his leadership, the other parties of a BJP-led formation may not agree to have him at the helm.

Nitish Kumar, chief minister of Bihar and representative of the Janata Dal (U) which was part of the BJP-led National Democratic Alliance (NDA) government, has already made clear his opposition to Modi in no uncertain terms. Nitish refused permission to Modi to campaign in Bihar and did not attend Modi's swearing-in – even if only for token value. Other partners of the former NDA (or whatever new alliance that the BJP may form) might have the same reservations. Odisha's Naveen Patnaik, who, like Modi is a bachelor and a third-term chief minister, is also gearing up for the race to the prime minister's office. Odisha has 21 seats in Lok Sabha, just under Gujarat's 26 seats. Though Tamil Nadu chief minister, Jayalalitha has unabashed admiration for Modi, the buzz goes that her preference for the prime minister's office would be Patnaik.

Thus, it is only in the event of BJP getting a majority on its own, i.e. 272 seats out of the total of 543 seats in the Lok Sabha, that Modi could become the executive head of the country without a hitch.

Historically though, the BJP has never won so many seats: the highest number hitherto, both in 1998 and 1999 was 182 seats.

Many with their ears to the ground feel that a strong sentiment for change is perceptible across the country. The common man is fed up of corruption and bad governance. People are also tired of continual political squabbles, deal-making and the appeasement of one segment of society or another. In these circumstances, people want a strong administrator who can effortlessly wield the reins of power. They also want energetic leaders and are not willing to be restricted by ideological constraints in their choices. 'We want somebody who can deliver results and not leaders whose only strength is to keep quiet,' says Sudhir Mishra, a young IT professional from Gurgaon.

'Things are seriously wrong across the nation and we want someone who can set things right very quickly. It does not matter to what political denomination he belongs,' says Anil Dass, a school teacher from Jabalpur.

It is due to this search for energetic leaders that people are rallying behind politicians as diverse as Jaganmohan Reddy in Andhra Pradesh, Mamata Banerjee in West Bengal, and Narendra Modi. Observers point out that slowly but surely, citizen apathy is on the wane. Electronic Voting Machine technology has further enthused more and more urban voters to exercise their franchise. 'Citizen movements have come up in many cities and even commercials like the one of a young man coming home after casting his vote and telling his wife that he has done *badi duty*, are appearing on TV,' points out Jayprakash Narayan of the Loksatta, a new party with political reform as its main agenda. Younger voters want change and they might be attracted to Narendra Modi, feel some analysts. Even in Gujarat, Modi's latest win is attributed to young voters who cast their franchise for the first time.

'In Andhra Pradesh, Jagan Reddy has such a strong support base, in spite of being in jail with so many charges of wrongdoings against him. Similarly, the fact that Modi presided over Gujarat when unprecedented riots hit the state is not something that will go against him, except among the minorities and the more liberal sections,' agrees a Congress leader.

Quick to grasp the popular mood, Modi has been assiduously positioning himself as an agent of change and a strong administrator to boot. In fact, over the last ten years he has been able to create the image among some, that the Gujarat riots did not escalate out of control only because of him!

Anil Haldar, a Hyderabad restaurant-owner, incredulously told me that the law of the jungle had prevailed till Modi had come along and set things right. One class XII student listed Narendra Modi as his role model. 'Gujarat was a backward place before Modi came along,' the young lad told me. 'He brought water to the farms and rapidly industrialized the state.' Obviously, Modi has been able to project a larger-than-life image for himself, part-fact, part-fiction: a branding that will surely help him in the race to South Block.

The neo-middle class, those millions whose incomes increased over two decades of economic reforms – might also be Modi's target. In fact, Modi's third successive victory in Gujarat is attributed partly to the emergence of this group.

In all the three assembly elections in Gujarat (2002, 2007, and 2012), the BJP garnered 50 per cent of all the votes polled. While the polarization of Hindu votes was the cause in 2002, the same was not the case at the last election in 2012.

While the Hindu vote forms part of the overall tally of the BJP in 2012, another is the vote of the neo-middle class who, benefitting from the reforms, are enjoying better lifestyles.

Of course, it is impossible to figure out to what extent the BJP votes are attributable to the neo-middle class and to the political ideology of the party.

Says Monotosh Sinha, a corporate manager from Bihar who now lives in Mumbai: 'I can discern a change in the voting behaviour of the neo-middle class. In the good old days, people used to vote on the basis of castes. But nowadays, many are going to work, say, outside Bihar in prosperous states like Punjab or Gujarat. When they visit home, they compare their towns with what they have seen in their workplace and seek change. Such people could vote on the basis of economic development and therefore potentially for Modi.'

This is true not only of white-collar employees from states like Bihar, but also of skilled and unskilled labourers who find opportunities in other states. Ramanand Mishra, a bank manager from Bihar who now works in Hyderabad, agrees. 'Voters – especially the upcoming middle class – are looking at other parameters. Though Nitish Kumar has been voted into power for the second time on the basis of his good economic performance, voters are now demanding more. This is why the name of Modi is being mentioned. Many feel that only Modi can better the performance of Nitish Kumar. But as of now, he is untested in Bihar.' Mishra further speculates that this could be the reason why Nitish opposes, tooth-and-nail, the entry of Modi into Bihar for campaigning.

It is easy to see that the neo-middle class are more likely to fall to Modi's charms in states where the BJP already has a base, and where the Sangh parivar's philosophy has already struck roots. This would mean traditional BJP states like Madhya Pradesh and Rajasthan, where there is equal fervor for the Ram Janmabhoomi movement as in Gujarat, if not more. 'Already a believer in BJP's philosophy, the perception of rapid economic growth under Modi will be a great mobiliser of votes among the neo-middle class in a place like this,' says Amit Gupta, a doctor from Ratlam in Madhya Pradesh. On the other hand and in spite of concurrence on Modi's good economic performance in Gujarat, votes may not get diverted to him in states where the BJP philosophy has failed to entrench itself. 'We admire what Gujarat has become under Modi, but to vote for him? That's out of question. The negative scorecard of his communal record outweighs his performance on the economic front', says Chandreyee Ghose, a professional commenting on the view held by most of Kolkata's middle class.

In states like Odisha, Modi might fare better amongst the neo-middle class but is unlikely to get unqualified acceptance. BJP, which had been in government along with the BJD in Odisha, was edged out by Naveen Patnaik when he won the last election all alone.

I remember that after Gujarat 2002, VHP president Praveen Togadia had declared that Odisha would be the next station for his organization. Although Odisha had seen anti-Christian violence, the VHP could not make much headway in the state. Togadia told me: 'Hindus in Odisha are very religious-minded but their religiosity does not make them anti-Muslim or anti-Christian.' Further, the consumerist culture has not taken root so deeply in the state, a Gujarat model of development could hold the people spellbound.

However, Karnataka is a different story. Kumara Guru, a young management professional working in Chandigarh, was surprised to find a huge following for Narendra Modi in his hometown Bengaluru during the New Year holiday. 'Karnataka is a BJP state and the neo-middle class across the country favours him. But I was taken aback by the intensity of the support all the way down to Mysore, unlike in states like Punjab etc. where the BJP is a marginal player.

A quick analysis shows that there are 135 seats for the Lok Sabha in the saffron-strong states of Gujarat, Rajasthan, Madhya Pradesh, Jharkhand, Chattisgarh, Karnataka, and Goa. It is here that Modi will be a strong contender in the polls and attract the young and the neo-middle class. In the 168 Lok Sabha seats in Bihar, Maharashtra, and UP, he will be a player, albeit not a significant one. These are states that BJP has never won on its own and has, in the past, ruled in alliance with other parties. In a state like UP, Mulayam Singh and Mayawati are as polarizing as Modi. In the remaining 140 seats spread across a wide array of states like West Bengal, Tamil Nadu, Andhra Pradesh, and Assam, conventional wisdom has it that Modi is unlikely to have any impact.

One of Modi's main support bases is big business houses. In the last five years, and more rapidly over the last three, corporates have converted to the Modi cause. What began as engagement with a government that offered attractive incentives in a state with a surplus of power and a labour-trouble-free reputation, grew into a veritable Modi mania.

In 2009, before the last general elections, some top industrialists had publicly voiced the view that Modi would make a good prime minister. This was seen as unprecedented. Generally, businessmen keep their political preferences under wraps and prefer to fund every political party.

'I think businessmen see in Modi a political CEO. As a rule, businessmen want a clear line of control. They are not comfortable dealing with coalitions under whom decision-making is on a seesaw. More than anything else, they want promises to be delivered on,' says economic and political commentator, Paranjoy Guha Thakurta. More importantly, businessmen in India have a desire to see a stable government with stable policies, led by someone who is also pro-business. But a BJP insider and Modi-skeptic says that big business can only contribute money, not organize votes. Furthermore, a section of society has begun to feel that Modi has become too 'autocratic.'

Another top businessman has stated that 'he is great for business, but he is not willing to listen to an alternative viewpoint and this is a problem'.

The wealthy Gujarati community also wants to see 'our man' as *bada pradhan* (Gujarati for prime minister). There is the widespread feeling in Gujarat that back in history, the position of prime minister had been denied to whom they thought was the most deserving candidate: Sardar Vallabhbhai Patel, the 'iron man' who had helped integrate the country. Many Gujaratis see in Modi a 'chote Sardar'; one who can keep the country intact and take the Patel dream forward. The fact that Delhi is ruled by the family of Jawaharlal Nehru, whose accession as the first prime minister of independent India denied Patel his chance, strengthens the resolve of the Gujaratis to install Modi in South Block. It is not surprising then that Modi himself likes to be called 'chote Sardar'.

'The Gujarati diaspora and businessmen are spread across the country. They will spare no effort to make Modi the prime minister and contribute everything that they can to place him in the number one slot,' says a Gujarati businessman.

But what kind of a prime minister will Narendra Modi make?

Considering that Modi has been chief minister of one state, even if for three terms, there are no easy answers to that question. His last engagement in national affairs, as a secretary of the BJP, was over a dozen years ago.

But one thing is clear: Narendra Modi will provide a complete contrast to Manmohan Singh. Quiet, virtually silent, Manmohan Singh, shares with Modi a rural background, but has read at top universities of the world and had huge international exposure as finance minister, governor of RBI, and finance secretary to the Government of India. Modi does not have the benefit of all this experience. But unlike Manmohan, Modi is a dyed-in-the-wool politician. Also unlike Manmohan, whose image is that of a prime minister continually making compromises, Modi is voluble and firm.

In fact, some analysts snigger, rather sarcastically, that Manmohan is not prime minister of India but prime minister to Empress Sonia. Playing second fiddle to anyone is not Modi's nature, though he is also known to make compromises when they seem practical.

If he becomes prime minister, Modi will also be strikingly different from Atal Behari Vajpayee, the only BJP man to occupy the high office till now. As BJP organizer Govindacharya said (in a remark for which he had to pay a political price) Vajpayee was a *mukhauta* (mask) for the hard-line party, the man who represented the soft, acceptable face of the BJP. In fact, it was only because of the liberal image of Vajpayee that BJP got the support of other parties in the NDA when it came to power. It is well known that hardliner Advani, under whom the party launched Ram Janmabhoomi, had to make way for Vajpayee. Atal was a great public orator and so is Modi. But the nature of their oratory is different. 'Vajpayee's oratory was humorous, often poking fun at himself, full of words of wisdom and very enjoyable to hear, but Modi's oration is fully charged and often hits opponents below the belt,' says a journalist. 'They are as different as chalk and cheese and this will be reflected in their policies,' says RSS sympathizer Arvind Bosmia. 'Though Vajpayee also took some hard decisions like nuclear testing, Modi's policies will, going by what he has done in Gujarat, be bold and decisive.'

P.V. Narasimha Rao, prime minister of India from 1991 to 1996, was seen as a master of compromises who managed to pull through with a minority government for five years. Having failed to stop the demolition of Babri Masjid, Rao was not seen as decisive. And yet, he was the man during whose term liberalization was initiated.

Modi and Narasimha Rao bear as little resemblance to each other as Modi and Rajiv Gandhi.

Pleasant and well-spoken, though without much knowledge of political machinations, Rajiv was moored in the values of cosmopolitanism and his main advisers consisted of rich urbanites with a background similar to his.

Whenever Modi is criticized for the 2002 riots and his 'action-reaction' statements (the riots being a reaction to the Godhra train carnage), his friends point to a similar statement made by Rajiv Gandhi, after his mother Indira Gandhi was assassinated. On the second day of the anti-Sikh riots, Rajiv Gandhi is quoted as saying: 'When a big tree falls, the earth under it shakes'. The statement drew a lot of flak.

But that is where the similarity ends. While Rajiv Gandhi had, in a way, the prime minister's job thrust on him when Indira Gandhi died, Modi is a man who has been working his way assiduously up to the chair of prime minister.

Narendra Modi also cannot be compared to Jawaharlal Nehru, the first prime minister of India who got the top job after fighting for independence and spending time in jail for the cause. Besides the great dissimilarity in family backgrounds, education, and circumstances, Nehru and Modi did, of course, belong to two different eras. In fact, Nehru was already prime minister when Modi was born.

There is also little similarity between the two Gujaratis: Morarji Desai and Narendra Modi. They, too, came from entirely different backgrounds.

Desai hailed from prosperous south Gujarat which has strong connections with Mumbai. Modi hails from north Gujarat which is distinctly backward and has an entirely different ethos.

The politics of the two cannot be compared either. Morarji was an old Congressman cast in the Gandhian mould, whereas Modi did his apprenticeship in the RSS, whose world view has nothing in common with that of the Congress. The only thing common among them is extreme stubbornness.

Modi and Lal Bahadur Shastri both came from underprivileged backgrounds. But Shastri was low-key and it was because of this that he was nominated by Nehru as his successor. Modi is anything but low-key.

If there is any prime minister of India that Modi can be compared to, it is Indira Gandhi. She began as an underdog, but powered her way to the top, destroying the old syndicate that controlled Congress politics up to then. She was also a demagogue, capable of decisive action and a great maneuverer. Ditto for Modi. Indira too connected with the masses directly, bypassing the political executive. The same is the case with Modi in Gujarat, the only place where he has been tested so far. Just as Congress candidates got elected to the Lok Sabha by virtue of their being Indira Gandhi's representatives, similarly in Gujarat, many BJP candidates have got elected by being Modi's *manas* (Modi men).

Both evoke fear in party men: like Modi, Indira too did not allow party colleagues to take her for granted.

But here, the similarity between the two ends. Indira's world view was governed by the socialist world: she coined the term *'garibi hatao'*, she nationalized banks, coal mines, insurance, and petroleum companies. She removed privy purses and made a distinctive impression on tribals and women who counted her as somebody who would keep their interests in mind.

Narendra Modi, in contrast, is the darling of the industrialists and the business class, besides the Hindu-inclined sections of society. After breaking up with Pakistan, even her political opponents hailed Indira: Atal Behari Vajpayee compared her with Mother Durga. Unfortunately for Modi, he has no comparable fans in parties opposed to him.

Strangely enough and in some ways, Modi can be compared with Vishwanath Pratap Singh, who was prime minister for less than a year. Coming in from relative obscurity, V.P. Singh rode in as the anti-establishment crusader against corruption, just after the Bofors scandal broke out. The same is the case with Modi: he has also positioned himself as the man who will dismantle the establishment to set up a new order. Shortly after taking over as the prime minister, V.P. Singh, in a bold move, initiated massive social engineering by trying to implement the Mandal commission recommendations. He failed and lost power, but successive governments had to contend with his move and reservations for other backward castes (OBC) had to be put in place. Modi is also the type of leader who might try to propose radical reforms. Whether he fails or not is an entirely different issue.

In the final analysis, it may be premature to predict whether Modi will become prime minister or not, but it is a near certainty that he will export himself to Delhi. He already announced it by telling Gujarati newspersons after his election victory that from now onwards, he would speak in Hindi and not in his native Gujarati.

The ambition became more explicit when, after a fresh swearing-in, Modi hailed:'*Bharat Mata Ki Jai.*' And his constituents enthusiastically responded:'*Dekho dekho kaun aya, Bharat ka Sher aya.*'

From now on, Modi will be ensconced in a new bullet-proof office in Gandhinagar rather symbolically named'North Block'. From here, Modi will train his guns on South Block in New Delhi, hoping to conquer it in the not-too-distant future.

2

Son of the RSS

He was home after thirty-seven years, but not for good. The golden jubilee of his alma mater, B.N. High School, had brought Narendra Modi back in 1999 – if only for a few hours – to Vadnagar, an ancient Harappan site and now a small town in northern Gujarat. As BJP's general secretary, he was in a hurry to rush back to Delhi to attend to important party matters. But Narendra had none of the airs of a big man when he landed at the premises of the school on Station Road. He touched the feet of his teachers and surprised his Sanskrit teacher Prahladbhai Patel by effortlessly asking after the latter's children by name.

Narendra had left Vadnagar in 1967 at the age of seventeen. He had left in a huff and the general belief is that he did so when his parents brought his wife home for consummation of a marriage that had taken place many years ago. Narendra wanted to do something in life and did not want to be locked in domesticity. He had made up his mind many years ago. The growing lad would not accept this child marriage. But family pressure was such that he had no other way but to leave Vadnagar. (Narendra himself never talks about the marriage though, in the last few years, interviews of his wife Jashodaben have appeared in sections of the press. She was later a primary school teacher in a village in Banaskantha district and has since retired). Located 112 kilometres away, Ahmedabad was the natural choice.

There, Narendra sought refuge with his uncle who ran a canteen at the main bus station of the Gujarat State Road Transport Corporation. Uncle gladly employed the nephew and soon Narendra was at the cashier's till, issuing bills and collecting payments. Among those who frequented this canteen was a RSS worker, Ambalal Khosthi. The swayamsevak was mighty impressed by the efficient ways of the manager who handled the front office of the canteen and even more pleased to learn that this young lad had been attending RSS shakhas in his native Vadnagar. Even as the friendship between Khosthi and Narendra blossomed, the latter decided to strike out on his own and set up a tea stall close by.

Brewing up pots of tea was no big deal for Narendra – his father Damodardas ran a tea stall at Vadnagar railway station. Young Narendra assisted his father in the morning, when several passenger trains passed that way, before running off to school. Damodardas had six children. Although his main business was of selling edible oil, he ran the tea stall to earn an additional income. Narendra had, from a young age, baulked at the idea of following in the footsteps of his father and had always wanted to be active in public affairs. In the mid-'60s, considering the stratum of society he came from, this was a tall order. Sons of *ghanchis* (oilmen) of a lower caste like Narendra, followed the traditional occupation of their fathers. Little wonder that at the young age of eight, he joined the bal-shakha of the RSS. He would run to the bal-shakha every day after school because that allowed him to participate in something more interesting than his dreary daily life of serving tea at the railway station and going to school.

School did not hold much interest for Narendra, who was an average student. But extra-curricular activities like dramatics and debating excited him. In 1965, he acted in a school play titled *Jogidas Khuman*, based on the life of an outlaw of the Saurashtra area who turned a saint under the influence of Swaminarayan Bhagwan. Narendra was originally given the lead role. But since his physique was slight, his role was changed to that of Vajesinh Maharaj, the royal whose territory is marauded by Jogidas. The next year – 1966 – saw Narendra take up the role of a soldier in a play called *Haryali No Hatyaro*. The play was based on the Chinese aggression of India and Narendra showed patriotic fervour while enacting his role. In school, he was also interested in leadership roles and stood for the election of class representative. Bigger boys bullied him but Narendra would not be cowed down. One of his teachers remembered that he was a 'frank, fearless boy' but 'extremely self-willed'. The latter is a trait he has retained. Among other incidents, old-timers recollect that during the Indo-Pakistan conflict of 1965, Narendra was charged up and voluble on how all Pakistanis should be decimated. He was also active in serving free tea to troops whose train would stop at Vadnagar station on their way from the Kutch border.

When Khosthi introduced him to the big bosses of the local outfit of RSS in Ahmedabad, Narendra was thrilled. It was reciprocal: the seniors were equally pleased to meet a young man in whom they discerned potential. Although the RSS branch in Ahmedabad at Hegdewar Bhawan in the middle-class area of Maninagar had been around for many years, the organization did not have a vast following. Like most of the RSS leadership, Lakshmanrao Inamdar, a Maharashtrian Brahmin, had opened the Ahmedabad unit in the early 1950s when the city was still part of Bombay Presidency and Gujarat was yet to be created (the demand for a Gujarati speaking state was realized in 1960).

But those were heady days of socialism; even though the Gujaratis, by nature, believed in free enterprise, there was nothing in the RSS that attracted them much. The RSS chugged on more like an underground organization. Vakil Saheb – as Inamdar was popularly called, because he earlier had practiced law – used to tour the state extensively setting up RSS shakhas. But progress was slow. Inamdar had other assistants like Nathulal Zagda, the prant pracharak of the RSS and another Maharashtrian Brahmin, Vasant Gajendragadkar, a lawyer at the Ahmedabad city civil courts. Narendra was very impressed with Inamdar who, he felt, had established the RSS branch office by making enormous personal sacrifices. Though Inamdar was quite senior, he became the young lad's mentor. Thirty years later in 2001, Modi penned a biography of Inamdar, titled *Jyoti Punj*, which was released by then Prime Minister Atal Behari Vajpayee. Among other things, the book recalled how Inamdar donned his black robes to fight legal battles for compatriots who had been jailed in the aftermath of Mahatma Gandhi's assassination. During the earlier protests against the Nizam, Inamdar himself had had a taste of a few months in jail. In RSS circles, many still consider Modi to be the *manas putra* of Inamdar, the man who had influenced him the most during his formative years.

Very soon Narendra, who had no permanent abode, shifted to the RSS headquarters as an assistant. 'It was a momentous move because this shift gave Narendra an identity and a sense of purpose in life. Now for the first time he was not alone, he was part of a bigger family. This, I reckon, went a long way in shaping his personality,' says a RSS karyakarta who was with Narendra in those days. 'Narendra's otherwise tough life, too, became a wee bit easier.'

It was a small premise with about ten persons in six rooms. Besides being inducted into the organization and since Narendra was an apprentice, he was also required to chip in on menial tasks. This included making tea for the denizens (all of whom were pracharaks), sweeping and swabbing the rooms. Narendra was so influenced by Lakshmanrao Inamdar that he volunteered to launder his clothes as well. Since he was also in charge of the RSS in Maharashtra and Goa, Inamdar's visits to Ahmedabad were irregular. But whenever he came, Narendra was at his beck and call. Arvind Bosmia, an RSS-watcher and himself a right winger says that Modi was welcomed with open arms into the organization not only because he seemed to be committed, but also because he came from a backward class. 'The RSS was seen as an organization run by Brahmins. This had restricted its attractiveness to other castes. The organization wanted to overcome this by welcoming more people from the lower castes. Modi was a prize catch and so was Shankersinh Vaghela who became his bête noire many decades later,' says Bosmia.

Around the time that Modi was being wooed by the RSS, the organization was seeking to upscale its presence in Ahmedabad. In December 1968, a huge RSS rally was held in the city and addressed by its top national leaders. This had the result of raising the temperature among the 'Hindu'-inclined sections of the community, although there was nothing that the top leadership referred to other than the atrocities on Hindus at the time of the partition. In September 1969, Ahmedabad (which had a history of communal trouble dating back to 1714) saw its worst-ever communal trouble. It was sparked by a series of incidents that included the desecration of the Koran by a Hindu superintendent of police. A few months later, a police inspector showed similar disrespect to the Ramayana on Janmasthami day. Jana Sangh MP, Balraj Madhok made the situation worse by arriving in the city and making statements that would not exactly promote amity. The formation of a Hindu Dharma Rakshak Samiti added fuel to the fire. A clash between sadhus of the Jagannath temple and thousands of Muslims who had gathered for the annual Urs at a nearby dargah was the spark that led to a communal conflagration that left 660 dead. Most of them were Muslims. These incidents must have had some impact on Narendra's young, impressionable mind.

Till date, Narendra Modi never gets drawn into such a conversation. The Justice Jaganmohan Reddy committee set up by the government to investigate the riots blamed it on extreme factions of organizations like the Jana Sangh and RSS but did not name anyone. But a then-serving senior police officer says: 'The government led by Gandhian Hitendra Desai had told the police not to use rifles. Thus, the police was unable to contain the disturbances. The riots were terrible. Even Ahmedabad railway station was full of dead bodies, because passengers alighting from trains were killed. Inept police action worsened the riots.'

The 1970s were the beginning of politically tumultuous times in Gujarat and Ahmedabad. The split of the Congress left the party led by Indira Gandhi in a considerably weakened position what with a large number of leaders and workers joining the other Congress (called Congress organization) led by the home-bred Morarji Desai. As usual, internal wrangles and factionalism worsened the situation. In July 1973, a relatively young Chimanbhai Patel forced the leadership to change its existing chief minister Ghanshyam Oza and anoint him as the boss. His appointment coincided with a drought in Gujarat and soon prices of essentials – like food-grains and edible oils were sky-rocketing. Public anger began to mount and soon it was vented by students of LD Engineering College in Ahmedabad. What brought matters to a head was the increase in the mess bill for hostellers from ₹70 a month to ₹100 in December 1973. Students protested and soon the campus agitation spilled to the streets. It struck a chord with the common man who, too, was suffering. Groundnut oil prices had soared to ₹9.50 per litre from ₹7 per litre the year before. Cries of 'Chiman Chor' rent the air, even as students raised slogans that it was because the chief minister was accepting cuts from the *telia rajas* (the groundnut kings who controlled the trade), that he was allowing the increase in prices of groundnut oil. Joined by students from other colleges of Gujarat University, crowds marched to the homes of ministers demanding their resignation. Violence broke out, buses were hijacked and the students resorted to bandhs and fasts. The army was called in and the Maintenance of Internal Security Act (MISA) was invoked. The police swung into action and many were killed in firings. The trouble spread to all major towns in the state and forty cities came under curfew. On their part, student leaders made strenuous efforts to keep political parties away from the movement. But sensing an opportunity, parties tried their best to cash in on the riots. In February 1974, Indira Gandhi dismissed the Chimanbhai Patel government and imposed President's Rule. Chimanbhai himself was expelled from the party. But this did nothing to ease the situation and the students announced a *Navnirman* movement for reconstruction of society. One of the parties interested in becoming part of the movement was the Jana Sangh. Narendra Modi who, by now, had been given charge of looking into the affairs of the Akhil Bharatiya Vidyarthi Parishad (ABVP) in Gujarat by his RSS bosses, started frequenting the public meetings of the leaders of the student movement. 'I know that he participated in some of the many relay fasts organized by the students,' says Hanif Lakdawala, a psychiatrist and social activist. But Narendra was unable to break into the inner group because the student leaders had an aversion to representatives with political affinities. However, he continued to keep a close watch on the movement. By now Jayaprakash Narayan, who was raising his voice against the functioning of the Indira Gandhi government, came to Ahmedabad to gain a first-hand impression of the situation on the ground. Narendra Modi remembers that Gujarat proved an inspiration for Jayaprakash Narayan's movement in Bihar and 'Gujarat ka Anukraran' was a popular phrase in that state. Morarji Desai went on an indefinite fast in March 1975 demanding the state assembly, which was in suspended animation, be dissolved and fresh elections be ordered. Feeling the heat of the opposition, Indira Gandhi had no choice but to comply and elections were declared for June 1975. In his days overseeing the ABVP, Narendra may have pursued a college education. 'I have seen his post-graduate degree. He is an MA in political science from Gujarat University. He had himself shown it to me in the mid-nineties,' says senior journalist Deepal Trivedie, who is not known to be a fan of his. 'But it is true that in all these years, I have never met anyone who taught or studied with him,' she adds. The website of the BJP's Gujarat unit also mentions that Narendra Modi is an MA in political science, though there are no details available about where he graduated from. The site also says that he left his hometown and came to Ahmedabad charged with 'political fervour and nationalist spirit' and approached the RSS office. 'He did his BA as a private student. I know some professors whose classes he had attended as an MA student, but I am not sure that he finished his post-graduation,' says a leading academician.

In the elections of June 1975, the Congress was routed and a non-Congress coalition government was formed. It was led by Babubhai Jasabhai Patel of the Kisan Mazdoor Lok Paksh (KMLP). The KMLP was a party spawned by Chimanbhai Patel who, after being thrown out of the Congress, was able to sell to the electorate the line that he had taken money from the *telia rajas* but it was for Indira Gandhi's election chest and not for himself.

However, Chimanbhai himself lost the election and the government was formed with the assistance of the Congress (organization) of Morarji Desai which won the lions' share of seats. The government, which was called the Janata Morcha sarkar, assumed office on 18 June, eight days ahead of the Emergency. This had an interesting ramification because when the Emergency was declared, the newly-appointed government refused to fully cooperate with the central government.

The Jana Sangh and the RSS opposed the Emergency tooth-and-nail and detailed all swayamsevaks to pitch in. However, their efforts faced a setback because all major leaders of the organization were ordered to be arrested and even the Gujarat government had to comply. Narendra had been assigned to work with Keshavrao Deshmukh, but the latter was arrested. By Narendra Modi's own account, the RSS boss of Gujarat, Nathalal Zagda, also faced arrest. But when the police came calling, Modi scooted away on his two-wheeler with Zagda on the pillion. At the time, Narendra himself was too small a functionary to be arrested by the cops. He took full advantage of this and sent a lady from a sister organization to go to the police station where Deshmukh was being held, before being taken to prison. On his person, Deshmukh had some documents pertaining to the future course of action of the RSS in Gujarat. Owing to the fact that the enforcement of the Emergency was not so rigorous in Gujarat, the lady was able to meet the RSS leader and get hold of the documents. Narendra Modi was always good at collecting and disseminating information and this became his work during this period. During the first few months of the Emergency, the young man got pamphlets and other literature pertaining to the excesses in north India, as well as material related to the Constitution of India and other legal matters, printed secretly. He also loaded them in trains leaving Ahmedabad for other cities. This was done covertly by avoiding the railway police who kept guard at stations. In his blogs, Modi himself has recollected that he also managed to dodge the police and convene confidential meetings in the Maninagar area of Ahmedabad. His other activities included identifying people who could support families of swayamsevaks who had gone underground or had been caught by the police. 'Opportunity may be a wrong word to use, but the Emergency provided a platform for Narendra Modi to prove his mettle. With all the bosses in jail or underground, a lot more work came his way. In normal circumstances his seniors would have probably taken on the burden,' says a BJP leader who does not want to be named. A posting on a blog site called Narendra Modi, which seems to be approved by him, says that in the course of the Emergency, Prabhudas Patwari (a Gandhian who later became governor of Tamil Nadu) called Narendra to his home and introduced him to George Fernandes. The latter, who was in disguise and was being hunted by the police, had sought assistance from an RSS leader. Narendra Modi organized a meeting between George Fernandes and RSS leader Nanaji Deshmukh, who also was underground. At the meeting, where Narendra was present, the socialist sought the help of Nanaji and the RSS for a violent plan of action to overthrow the Indira Gandhi government. But Nanaji understood the futility of violence and declined to help. A few months later, George Fernandes was arrested for the Baroda dynamite case. Besides these encounters and posing as a family member, Narendra Modi also visited Bhavnagar jail where Jana Sangh leader Shankersinh Vaghela was jailed. If he had been recognized as an RSS functionary, he would have been jailed too.

Gujarat had become a hub of anti-Emergency activities and Indira Gandhi was worried. Instability in the Jan Morcha government, rumoured to have been catalyzed by the Congress headquarters, offered her a golden opportunity: in March 1976, it was dismissed. Immediately, President's rule was imposed. Though it was lifted nine months later, political maneuvering in the interim period made it possible for a Congress chief minister to be installed in Gujarat again. Since Indira Gandhi did not want a known leader, she anointed the virtually unknown Madhavsinh Solanki as the new chief minister. A police officer who was an aide of the governor at that time has an interesting tale to narrate. He says that Solanki was so unknown that he had to make a Herculean effort to locate and contact him. 'Ultimately, we found him in the Memnagar area of Ahmedabad and told him that he was being appointed as chief minister,' the police officer says. Though Solanki's tenure did not last too long – the government fell after the Janata Party came to power in Delhi, heralding the end of Emergency – he was to create history in Gujarat. He achieved this by unveiling a new strategy because of which the Congress won two successive elections in 1980 and 1985, by a record majority. This is a record that even Narendra Modi has not been able to better.

It is doubtful whether Jinabhai Darji ever had a long, heart-to-heart chat with Narendra Modi in his lifetime. If the two had talked they would have found many things in common and many others, on which they would have vehemently differed. Hailing from southern Gujarat, Jinabhai belonged to a backward community. As his last name suggests, tailoring was the traditional profession of his family. But Jinabhai was influenced by Mahatma Gandhi and this made him join the freedom movement and the Congress party.

Later, as Jinabhai rose in the party, he also began to influence the affairs of the party. But when the Congress party split in 1969, he did not join Morarji Desai who also belonged to the same southern Gujarat region. Instead, he remained with Indira Gandhi, reckoning that under her, members of lower castes would prosper. In 1972, after winning the election to the post, he became the president of the Gujarat Congress. Jinabhai had his own theory about Gujarat politics. He believed that upper castes like Brahmins and Baniyas along with Patels, held hegemony over Gujarati society in much the same way as the Congress party. He believed that this was an unreliable combination because these castes were against social justice and many of them had crossed over to the Congress (organization). Jinabhai conjured up a new caste combination of KHAM that could form the new support base for the party. KHAM stood for Kshatriya, Harijan, Adivasi, and Muslim which were hitherto un-empowered sections of the Gujarati community. Together, they formed 60 per cent of the population of Gujarat and could become an unbeatable combination. It was on Jinabhai's advice that Indira Gandhi appointed Madhavsinh Solanki (a Kshatriya of lower social denomination) as chief minister, even as Jinabhai (who preferred to do party work and not join the government) was appointed chairman of the implementation committee of Indira's 20-point programme. The Patels were kept out of the Congress government. The Solanki government was short-lived because it was dismissed by the Janata government that took charge in New Delhi after the Emergency. Babubhai Jashbhai Patel became the chief minister once again in 1977 and continued till 1980. When there were elections to the Vidhan Sabha in 1980, Madhavsinh Solanki returned to power with a huge majority for the Congress. The party won 141 seats out of the total 182 in the assembly.

The KHAM strategy yielded grand results. Egged on by Darji and to the chagrin of the hitherto important castes whose members were being kept out of the power matrix in a conspicuous way, the Solanki government continued to empower the lower castes. The first signs that this strategy would succeed emerged in 1978, barely a year after Indira Gandhi was ousted from power. Jinabhai Darji was able to mobilize a crowd of one lakh for a public meeting of Indira Gandhi in Surat, which was the constituency from where the prime minister of the time, Morarji Desai, had been elected.

In 1981, with a view to consolidate the KHAM base, the Madhavsinh Solanki government accepted the recommendations of the Bakshi Commission of 1972 that envisaged 10 per cent reservations for other backward castes in admissions to educational institutions. This would be in addition to the 7 per cent reservations for scheduled castes, and 14 per cent for scheduled tribes. The acceptance of the report became the mobilizing point for a violent anti-reservation agitation that erupted in parts of Gujarat. The affected regions included Ahmedabad, Nadiad and Vadodara. The riots went on for two months and surprisingly, they soon took on an anti-Dalit hue. Many Dalits were killed, their hamlets torched and property destroyed. Far more intense anti-reservation riots took place in 1985, this time degenerating into Hindu-Muslim confrontations in Ahmedabad. It all began in the second week of February 1985 when in the run up to the state assembly elections, the Solanki government raised the number of seats reserved for other backward castes in post-graduate educational institutions from 10 per cent (determined in 1981) to 28 per cent. This effectively hiked overall reservations to 49 per cent. The rationale of the hike lay in a convoluted logic: a household survey commissioned by the Rane Commission (that had been set up to smoothen the findings of the earlier Bakshi Commission) had found that 28 per cent of the people of Gujarat was below the poverty line. The Rane Commission had conducted this survey after changing the methodology of identifying backwardness from caste to income and occupation. The Solanki government accepted that reservations should be raised to 28 per cent and increased the reservation to OBC (as identified by castes) to this new, higher figure. This was done on the assumption that all the poor were actually OBCs and Dalits. But in reality, this was not so: there were many high castes who could be poor too.

This incensed the members of the upper castes who saw it as a thinly-veiled attempt to pander to voters ahead of the upcoming elections. Immediately, students of engineering and medical colleges launched agitations. They demanded a postponement of examinations and withdrawal of the quotas. Buses were burnt and stones pelted at schools and colleges. The agitation spread rapidly. To curtail the mobilization of students and contain the trouble, the government ordered that educational institutions be closed. They were reopened a month later. Now parents and guardians of students entered the fray and formed the Gujarat Vali Mandal. Language newspapers supporting the cause of agitating parents spread the message and fanned the agitation. The trouble then took on a communal hue. Major clashes flared up in the Dariapur area of Ahmedabad where Hindus and Muslims lived in equal proportion. The area was home to textile workers, who had been laid off by Ahmedabad's textile mills when the latter were rendered uneconomical by power looms which had sprung up 265 kilometres further south in Surat.

Along with the large numbers of anti-social elements in gambling dens and in the business of brewing illicit liquor in the old city, these frustrated mill workers too jumped into the fray.

The riots notwithstanding, and with 149 of the 182 seats, the Congress party romped home in the assembly elections. However, Madhavsinh Solanki had to make way for a new man. Amarsinh Chaudhary, a protégé of Solanki, became the chief minister in July 1985. The high command realized that anointing Solanki was a big risk because the upper castes reacted violently to his name. Amarsinh was a tribal from south Gujarat and the only tribal to be chief minister of Gujarat till date.

The rapid pace with which the Solanki–Darji duo tried to empower the backward classes at the cost of the upper castes who had until now held all positions of power, brought about changes at the grass-roots level. Though the immediate manifestation was the anti-reservation riots, the upper castes were searching for a party which would represent their interests. The Patels were the most active in this search for new empowerment. Though they were not an entirely homogeneous group, they were, more or less, an upcoming agrarian community. About five hundred years ago when the Patels had lived on the edges of villages in Saurashtra and northern Gujarat, their social status had been almost as low as that of tribals. Over time, there was slight improvement. By the time India became free, most of them were either landless cultivators or farmers owning small tracts of land. Land reforms in the 1950s brought them in possession of more land, and after the Green Revolution their income and economic status improved greatly. Many of them started businesses and some migrated overseas. Having arrived economically, the community began to look for political empowerment. With this objective in mind, in the early '70s, they hitched their fortunes to those of the Congress. A branch of the Patels who lived in central Gujarat were relatively better off than the Patels of Saurashtra and northern Gujarat. They had been empowered earlier: Sardar Vallabhbhai Patel, India's first deputy prime minister, was one such Patel.

With the advent of the Darji-Solanki duo and their anti-upper caste policies, the Patels found themselves at the receiving end. Numerically at over 20 per cent, they were technically only a middle caste. Unlike the Brahmins and Baniyas who had been empowered for long, the Patels were still in the process of acquiring higher educational qualifications, when Solanki's reservation policies were unveiled. This agitated the Patels to no end and they joined the anti-reservation movement in large numbers. Politically, they began to shift away from the Congress. The desire of the Patels to move away from the Congress coincided with the advent of the BJP. In its earlier avatar as the Jana Sangh, the party had made little headway in Gujarat but with the imposition of the Emergency, they merged with other parties like the Congress (Organization) to form the Janata Party which came to power in New Delhi after the Emergency. However, the party split over the issue of dual memberships of erstwhile members of the Jana Sangh, who wanted to remain RSS members even while being in the Janata Party. Now the Bharatiya Janata Party (BJP) took birth. This was a party in search of followers, while the Patels were in search of a party to articulate their cause. It was a perfect fit, but the match did not happen overnight. Slowly but surely, over a period of ten years, the Patels had to be wooed assiduously by the BJP. Along with the Patels, the numerically miniscule but otherwise influential Brahmin and Baniya communities also started aligning their fortunes with the new party. The BJP, which won 11 assembly seats – out of a total of 182 – in the elections in 1985, was able to increase its tally to 67 in the next elections of 1990. 'This was the result of our strategy and mobilization,' says Raju Dhruv, a BJP leader from the state.

Describing Gujarat in the 1980s, the blog on Narendra Modi says: 'In Gujarat, curfew became the most common word in the household directory. Brother against brother, communities against communities and vote bank politics became the norm.' It goes on to say that in this scenario, Narendra Modi – who had established himself not only as a dedicated worker but also as an efficient organizer – worked very hard for the RSS in this *battle of ideals*. For his admirers, Modi might have risen to the situation, but here is what a retired officer, who at the time was in charge of political intelligence, has to say: 'At the time, the RSS and BJP were not really considered important. Thus they were not on our radar. The government of the day was more bothered about dissidents in the Congress and erstwhile Congressmen who could regroup and pose a challenge to the establishment.' Journalist Sheela Bhatt, who had travelled to Ahmedabad from Mumbai to cover the riots in 1985, remembers meeting Modi. 'It was at the house of a RSS official. He was thin and looked small. He bore no resemblance to what you see now. Also, he was not so free with his opinions.' Bhatt adds that activists like Haren Pandya (Modi's minister who deposed against him after the 2002 riots) and Ashok Bhatt (another latter-day minister in Modi's government) were far more vociferous.

The BJP was formed in 1980. But having been decimated in the 1984 general elections, it faced a national crisis barely five years after its formation.

With the shadow of the assassination of Indira Gandhi looming large over the elections, the BJP could just win two seats in a house of 543. One of the seats was in Andhra Pradesh and the other was Mehsana in Gujarat. Party senior L.K. Advani later said that it was not Lok Sabha elections but a 'shok sabha' for Indira Gandhi. The party now realized that it would have to be more aggressive to expand fast: otherwise it would always be subject to the vagaries of external factors. The RSS, the parent organization of the BJP, had always believed that Hinduism was the glue that held India together and that the term 'Hindu' was broad enough to encompass the Christians, Sikhs, and Muslims of India. The reasoning was that in any case, most of the other religious groups had been Hindus earlier who had been converted. In 1986, Advani – who had served in the RSS in important positions before joining the Jana Sangh and the BJP – became the president of the party. He was given the mandate for putting the party on the fast track. Since the party was doing well in Gujarat, he started by consolidating BJP affairs in the state by co-opting the Patels into the party's fold aggressively. In the meantime, the Ram Janmabhoomi movement was taking shape. For the BJP, it seemed to bear good prospects to mobilize Hindus under a common platform across the nation. In Gujarat, this would form a second prong of the strategy to consolidate the party. Advani was looking for a good organizer, a zealous man who understood the philosophy of the RSS well. His choice fell on Narendra Modi who had stood out for his excellent skills at gathering information and managing people at the grass-roots level during the course of his work at the RSS. Modi was 37 years old and had been with the RSS for over a decade and a half. He was energetic and a good orator to boot. Accordingly and with Advani's recommendation, he was deputed to the BJP in 1987. If the first phase of Narendra's life had ended the day he joined the RSS, the second was now drawing to a close. Modi was now entering the more eventful and significant third phase of his life.

3

BJP's Master Planner

Gurcharan Singh, retired additional chief secretary of the Gujarat government, remembers a train journey from Ahmedabad to Mumbai circa 1991. Modi, whose name he had barely heard then, was travelling in the same compartment.

'To my utter surprise and at every station, a large number of people came to felicitate him. There was a big delegation of BJP workers even at Mumbai Central, where our journey ended,' the former officer recalls. 'I began to wonder who this man was and how come I was not familiar with him.'

Unknown to the movers and shakers of society, ever since 1987 when he was deputed to the BJP, Modi had come a long way. Given the impact of his work within a year of his entry, Narendra – now referred to as Modi by those who knew him – was promoted to general secretary of the Gujarat BJP. Among other things, his organizing a Nyay Yatra within a few months of joining, had won him acclaim in BJP circles.

'This was to demand justice for Hindu riot victims whom the pseudo-secular government was ignoring,' says RSS watcher Arvind Bosmia.

Two years later, Modi organized the Lok Shakti Yatra: a mobilization against the liquor mafia in the old city of Ahmedabad.

Excited at the performance of the new catch, Advani gave Modi the job of organizing the Gujarat leg of his now well-known Ram

Rath Yatra from Somnath to Ayodhya. Though Advani had decided to concentrate his efforts on Ram Janmabhoomi shortly after he became the chief of BJP in 1986, the plan was to consolidate the movement slowly. But V.P. Singh, who came to power at New Delhi as the head of a Janata Dal government supported from outside by the BJP, changed the game suddenly by introducing reservations for Other Backward Castes (OBCs) in government jobs. This was as per the ten-year-old Mandal commission report that was, till then, gathering dust. Unable to oppose reservations, yet not comfortable with them, since they would hit BJP's upper-class following, Advani hastily decided on a Rath Yatra to influence public discourse. This would serve to consolidate – or at least, aim at consolidating – Hindu votes which could benefit the BJP. That the yatra would culminate at Ayodhya was a given. But the story has it that it was Modi's idea that it should start at Somnath, located on the coast in Gujarat's Saurashtra region. It houses an ocean-front temple of Lord Shiva and the name Somnath is derived from it. The ancient Hindu place of worship, replete with riches, was attacked and destroyed by Mahmud Ghaznavi's marauding troops for the first time in 1026 AD. The temple was rebuilt many times, each time to be destroyed by Ghaznavi, who came all the way from Afghanistan to loot its fabulous treasures.

'Somnath is the living symbol of the assault on the temples and shrines of an ancient nation by Islamic invaders', Advani said, when launching his yatra on 25 September 1989.

After this cycle of destruction and reconstruction, the temple lay in ruins for hundreds of years till 1950, when its reconstruction was once again initiated by Sardar Patel as a symbol of resurgent Indian nationhood. The temple was rebuilt not by the government, but by funds from the people, which, according to Advani, was a manifestation of *lokshakti* (people's power) as opposed to *rajshakti* (official might). When embarking on his yatra on his 'rath', accompanied by Modi, Advani once again invoked the same people's power that had, in 1950, ensured the rebuilding of the Somnath temple. The choice of beginning the journey at Somnath and ending it at Ayodhya had another significance: it linked the Shaivaite tradition with the Vaishnavite tradition, thus seeking to unite Hindus of all spectrums.

At each one of the 600 villages in Gujarat the rath travelled through, large crowds greeted Advani. It was obvious that the yatra got off to a flying start. The route had been planned meticulously by Modi. Addressing about 50 wayside meetings, Advani (with Modi by his side) said that his journey to Ayodhya was not just about rebuilding a temple but also related to some fundamental questions: What is secularism? What is communalism? Can national integration be achieved by consistently pandering to minority communalism? And can governments reject the cult of minority-ism?

'Evoking the destruction and plunder of Somnath, which is part of the folklore of Gujarat, captured public interest and was thus a brilliant move,' says senior journalist, Rajiv Shah. 'But this yatra and the mobilization that followed it also resulted in casting the Muslim as the "other" and as the "enemy" of Hindus. This was to have long-term repercussions.'

Shah also points out how the yatra was marked by demonstrations of religious fervour and militancy and how, in some places, women had offered Advani tilak with their own blood.

Incidentally by 1990, the Congress government in Gujarat had been voted out of power and replaced by a coalition government comprising the Janata Dal and the BJP. Unlike at the Centre, the BJP was part of the government in Gujarat and had a sizeable number of ministers. The chief minister was Chimanbhai Patel – the same person who had been booted out of the office sixteen years ago – in the wake of the Navnirman movement. The BJP ministers of the government put their might into escorting the Rath Yatra through their area and perhaps even misused the government machinery for the purpose.

The Rath Yatra was to traverse 10,000 kilometres and culminate on Dussehra day at Ayodhya. But as is well known, Advani was arrested at Samastipur in Bihar on the orders of the then chief minister Laloo Prasad Yadav (with the tacit support of V.P. Singh). The BJP immediately withdrew support to the V.P. Singh government, making no bones about why it was doing so. Reduced to a minority, the government fell after a no-confidence motion in Lok Sabha a few days later.

Communal peace was shattered in Gujarat after the arrest of Advani and Hindu–Muslim clashes broke out. Though yet to be widely known, Narendra Modi then declared the last week of October as the 'week of determination.' Meetings were organized in hundreds of towns and villages by the Vishwa Hindu Parishad (VHP) to spread the cause of the temple in Ayodhya. Violence ensued and it is estimated that more than 200 people died in the clashes even as the Hindu–Muslim divide deepened.

When Rajiv Gandhi was still the prime minister a year earlier, i.e. in 1989, the VHP had stepped up its campaign on the issue of the Ram Temple.

After receiving official permission, a 'shilanyas', or a ceremony to lay a foundation stone, took place at the site adjacent to the Babri Masjid. The VHP, which was part of the Sangh (RSS) parivar, decided that a good way of mobilizing support from all across the nation would be to involve the masses in the programme. And what better way could there be than to convince them to make bricks to be used in the construction of the temple as kar seva? This mobilization required extensive penetration of rural areas by the BJP/VHP cadres and motivating people to participate in the Ram Temple movement. While this became the collective effort of the Sangh parivar across the country, one person in Gujarat played an extremely zealous role: Narendra Modi.

Modi began by touring small towns and cities to spread the message and recruit volunteers. He also inducted many of them into the BJP, thus increasing its membership steeply. Ram Shila pujas happened in hundreds of villages across Gujarat to 'worship' and 'sanctify' the bricks that had been made there for the Ram temple.

A total of 275,000 consecrated bricks reached Ayodhya from all over India. Although nobody has kept any record of the number of bricks from Gujarat, the numbers were sizeable. Many say that the mobilization from Gujarat – not only in villages, but in cities and towns too – was the most impressive effort after the freedom struggle. A notable point about this mobilization was that it cut across caste lines: lower-caste Hindus, including scheduled castes and tribals too, had participated in the movement.

Not even remote hamlets had been ignored. This had an important electoral impact: it led to the formation of a composite Hindu vote bank.

'In Gujarat, the Ram Janmabhoomi movement led to the breakdown of the KHAM alliance that the Congress had constructed. The Kshatriya, Harijan, and the Adivasi combined with the Patel, Brahmins and Banias,' says academician Vidyut Joshi.

A yatra preceding Advani's journey from Somnath to Ayodhya had passed through the tribal areas of north and central Gujarat. This was aimed at roping in the Adivasis – the tribals – whose faith was based on animism – into the idea of the Ram Temple.

In the aftermath of the Somnath–Ayodhya Yatra, Modi became an overpowering functionary of the BJP in Gujarat.

During one of my tours in Gujarat just before the 1991 elections, I was advised by the national BJP executives to treat Modi as a single-point source of information.

Handing over a sticker bearing Modi's coordinates, Jagdish Shettigar, the convener of the economic cell of BJP said: 'He runs the show there. He knows everything like the back of his hand. If you meet him, there is no need to engage with anyone else.'

A former top official of Gujarat's Intelligence department had something similar to narrate.

He says that Advani – though leader of the Opposition – had wanted to meet him to understand the ground situation in Gujarat. After seeking permission from the then chief minister Chimanbhai Patel, the official called on Advani at the Circuit House at Ahmedabad.'When I entered the room, I found not only Advani but Modi too. My orders were to talk to Advani, one-on-one. I indicated that to Advani. But Modi remained adamant and would not move,' the Intelligence officer says.

When Advani finally signalled to Modi to leave, he merely moved to a chair in another part of the large room. 'The body language of Modi indicated that he was obviously an inseparable part of Mr Advani's entourage and wielded enormous influence over the BJP president,' the officer recollects.

The success of Modi's efforts in organizing the Gujarat leg of the Somnath–Ayodhya Yatra soon earned him his first national assignment. The new BJP President Murali Manohar Joshi wanted to focus on Kashmir – where militancy was rampant since 1989 – to pump the party's prospects. An Ekta Yatra from Kanyakumari (the southern-most tip of India) to Srinagar on Republic Day 1992 was planned. Highly impressed by Modi's meticulous organization of the Ayodhya Yatra, Joshi requisitioned his services for planning the long Ekta Yatra too. Modi's job was to visit the places ahead of the yatra and sensitize and prepare the BJP workers to receive the Joshi entourage with huge crowds. When the yatra began from Kanyakumari on 11 December 1991, Modi was present with Joshi and continued with him all the way to Srinagar. Along the way, he addressed party workers and the crowds mobilized by them at wayside meetings.

From the blog on Modi:'Wherever he went he echoed the message of Shyama Prasad Mookerjee of unity above anything else. He asked for the death knell of"pseudo secularism and vote-bank politics".'

If Modi was one of the most important functionaries of BJP in Gujarat who operated largely from the shadows, there was another, equally important person. This functionary was the public face of BJP within the state: Keshubhai Patel.

Keshubhai was an old war-horse who had joined the Jana Sangh in 1952, the year it was founded. He had an even older association with the RSS. A farmer-turned-small-flour-mill-owner, Keshubhai lived in Rajkot. In 1965, most unexpectedly, came a turning point in his life.

The thirty-five year old was cycling home from an RSS shakha when he chanced upon a big crowd at the market place. A notorious extortionist was collecting 'hafta' from shopkeepers, abusing them as he did so. The bystanders just stood there watching. Keshubhai dismounting from the cycle, went to the extortionist and told him to stop. But when the extortionist refused, a furious Keshubhai (who had been a wrestler earlier) thrashed him. The extortionist never came back again. Two years later, when local body elections were held, the same shopkeepers requested Keshubhai to contest. Keshubhai did – and won. In 1969, he was elected president of the state unit of the Jana Sangh, which was virtually nonexistent at the time. In 1972, Keshubhai was elected MLA and in 1975, when the coalition Babubhai Jashbhai ministry came to power, Keshubhai was appointed irrigation and agriculture minister in the short-lived government. After the formation of the BJP in 1980, it was left to Keshubhai (along with another, old Jana Sangh leader, Shankersinh Vaghela) to set up the physical infrastructure of the party.

He rented a small office at ₹1100 per month in the Ellisbridge area of Ahmedabad, but the office had to be given up because the party did not have enough funds. It was then shifted to the old city of Ahmedabad. 'We were so cash-strapped in those days. Nobody took us seriously either. Nobody would even loan a car to us for use of top party leaders visiting from Delhi,' recollects a party member.

But given the reservations policy of the Congress government, within a few years things were to change.

As the upper classes gravitated towards BJP as a mark of protest to the reservations, the party under Keshubhai started expanding its influence in zila and taluka panchayats and began concentrating on various cooperative institutions like cooperative banks, credit societies, milk cooperatives, and agricultural produce market committees.

'The Rajkot municipal corporation was won by BJP in 1983 and the Ahmedabad municipal corporation in 1987. The BJP realized that the route to Gandhinagar went through local power structures that had to be won,' points out Raju Dhruv.

Keshubhai was an important part of the scheme not only because of his old loyalty to the cause but also because he was the visible face of the Patels whose loyalties were shifting, lock, stock and barrel, towards the BJP. The Patels comprise approximately 20 per cent of the population of Gujarat that has a total of 182 seats in the assembly.

From its initial tally of 11 MLAs in a house of 182 in 1985, the BJP was able to return 67 MLAs in 1990. The Congress had been decimated: its tally fell from a staggering 149 to merely 33. But the Janata Dal had 90 MLAs. So a coalition with the Janata Dal, led by Chimanbhai Patel, came to power in March 1990. Keshubhai Patel was a minister in this government. But after the arrest of Advani on 25 October 1990, the BJP pulled out of the government. Still, Chimanbhai's government did not fall, because the chief minister could steer MLAs away from the Congress.

At a later date, Chimanbhai himself joined the Congress and continued in power till he died in office in February 1994. In his second term, Chimanbhai showed visionary leadership and laid the foundation for the Narmada dam project. He ushered in the development of ports, refineries, and power plants and laid the base for a modern industrial Gujarat. Much of the credit for his work which fructified a decade later, was appropriated by Narendra Modi.

Meanwhile, the BJP juggernaut was rolling and rolling fast. In the next assembly elections in 1995, the BJP, on its own, won 121 seats out of the total 182. Its vote share jumped to 42.5 per cent up from 27 per cent in the previous elections. For the first time, the saffron party was in a position to form a government by itself. But power, as they say, corrupts and brings along its own problems. Though the BJP bosses in Delhi thought that they would make Keshubhai Patel the chief minister, there was another contender: Shankersinh Vaghela. BJP leaders were startled to discover that Vaghela actually had the support of a majority of 121 legislators. Narendra Modi, who knew Vaghela intimately since his RSS days in Ahmedabad, thought that the latter could not be trusted. Moreover, if the Patel card had to be played successfully, then it would make strategic political sense to anoint Keshubhai as the chief minister. Modi – who, by now, had established himself as the ears and eyes of the BJP high command, especially for Advani – prevailed.

He not only fancied himself as the organizational boss responsible for the victory of the party, but also believed that his innovative strategies and planning alone were responsible for the BJP win in the local body elections too.

Keshubhai became the chief minister of Gujarat on 14 March 1995. As soon as that happened, Modi started running the show from outside the government. Journalist Rajiv Shah says: 'Sometimes, he would come to Cabinet meetings. Once, he attended a meeting where bureaucrats were being addressed by the chief minister.'

According to academician Vidyut Joshi, this was the first time that Modi came to be recognized in the public eye as an important person. 'Before this and in public imagination, he was merely a cog in the wheel. What his position in the party was, I do not know,' says Joshi.

But interfering in government matters was not the only thing that Modi did. 'He systematically began weeding out Vaghela supporters from positions of importance. This had the result of reducing the Vaghela camp in numerical terms. But at the beginning of September 1995, Vaghela still commanded the support of 47 MLAs,' says a BJP leader not willing to be named.

Vaghela was incensed when in September Keshubhai appointed the chairmen of 42 government boards and corporations (traditionally a way of rewarding ruling party loyalists who are not ministers). None of the chosen were Vaghela men. Shankersinh saw the combined hand of Keshubhai and Modi (supported by Advani) in this move. He declared a rebellion and scooted with his 47 MLAs, in a chartered plane to Khajuraho in Madhya Pradesh. The BJP, known for its discipline, became the laughing stock of the country, as the group checked into a five-star hotel.

'The incident stunned the BJP central leadership who, all along, had been assured by Modi that the strength of Vaghela had been overestimated and not more than a dozen MLAs would go with Vaghela if push came to shove,' the BJP leader says.

Had the BJP leadership had its antennae up, it would have realized that Prime Minister Narasimha Rao, through his emissaries, was in touch with Vaghela and was encouraging him to rebel. Vaghela was being assured that he could break away and become chief minister with the help of Congress MLAs, of whom there were 45 in number.

But who was this Vaghela who threatened to steal the thunder from the Gujarat unit of BJP?

Born in 1940, Vaghela was a decade younger than Keshubhai and a decade older than Modi and belonged to a Kshatriya family that hailed from a village not far from Gujarat's capital Gandhinagar. Military matters interested him and in school, Vaghela was part of the NCC. A macho man, he came in contact with the RSS and was soon inducted into their ranks. A few years later he was sent to the Jana Sangh and made the organizing secretary of the party that existed only in name. During the Emergency, Vaghela had been in jail for seventeen months and when the Janata Party came into existence he had been one of the vice presidents. When the BJP was formed in 1980, Vaghela became the first president of the party in Gujarat and remained in the position right until 1991.

Simultaneously, Vaghela got introduced to national politics and became Lok Sabha MP from 1977-80. Later he became a Rajya Sabha MP from 1984-89 and then re-entered Lok Sabha in 1989 and 1991.

All this made Vaghela senior to both Keshubhai and Modi in public life and therefore when the party got a chance to select a chief minister, Vaghela assumed that he should be the natural choice. This was also because Vaghela felt that it was largely due to his efforts that the Kshatriya votes (that formed part of the KHAM coalition of the Congress) had been weaned away from the Congress. 'But Advani did not trust him,' says a senior BJP leader. 'Egged on by Modi, Vaghela was denied the top slot, despite having more support amongst MLAs.' Incidentally, Modi and Vaghela were very close at one time, both being non-Brahmins in a Brahmin-dominated RSS in Gujarat. Vaghela was also one of those named responsible for the demolition of the Babri Masjid by the Liberhans Commission, set up by the government to investigate the matter. While the Commission arraigns L.K. Advani as accused number 1, Vaghela is accused number 49. However, Vaghela denies that he had anything to do with the demolition. 'I had never been to Ayodhya before 2008. My name has been wrongly included,' he says.

On 7 October 1995, barely seven months after he took over, the government of Keshubhai was on the verge of falling and rendering the BJP powerless in Gujarat.

But Atal Behari Vajpayee saved the day. After Vaghela returned from Khajuraho, Vajpayee reassured him by showing him a post-dated resignation that he obtained from Keshubhai. He also promised Vaghela that although he could not assure him the chief minister's job, a liberal non-RSS candidate could be entrusted with the position. Vaghela agreed. Of course, Vaghela's suspension from the party immediately after he flew to Khajuraho, was also rescinded. A fortnight later, a Vajpayee favourite, Suresh Mehta, became chief minister. Mehta was close to Vaghela; a number of the latter's men became ministers.

Now, MLAs and ministers loyal to Vaghela began to be called 'Khajurias', an allusion to their outing to Khajuraho. The other MLAs and ministers were referred to as 'Hazoorias' or the loyalists who did *jee-hazoori* to the BJP central office.

Keshubhai was not pleased and laid the blame for all that had happened at the doors of Modi. Keshubhai was influenced by Sanjay Joshi, another RSS pracharak who, like Modi, had been deputed to the BJP.

An engineer from Maharashtra, Joshi felt that much of the organizational work for the victory, now being claimed by Modi, had been his own work. Liberal elements in the BJP's central office also felt that Modi was primarily responsible for the Vaghela fiasco and needed to be punished.

Thus, Modi was to be banished from the state. It is believed that as punishment, he was to be dispatched to Guwahati to be in charge of BJP's Assam affairs. Considering that the BJP had no presence whatsoever in Assam, it was to be a sort of 'kalapani' (punishment by exile) for him. But Modi's godfather Advani intervened vehemently: Modi was given charge of the party's affairs in Himachal Pradesh and posted in Delhi. Though he kept visiting his home state, the BJP ensured that Modi, would have nothing to do with the party affairs in Gujarat. But this proved to be another turning point in Modi's life. New Delhi opened up an entirely new vista for him and though intended as punishment, his sojourn here turned out to be a stepping stone for success.

Meanwhile in Gujarat, BJP hardliners were not pleased at the turn of events: the fact that they were outsmarted by Vaghela. Opportunity came knocking the following year, when the general elections were held. Vaghela and a couple of his supporters lost the polls.

'It is an open secret that the hardliners worked overtime to get Vaghela and his men defeated. But, they may have cut their noses to spite their faces because in the process the BJP tally in Lok Sabha fell,' says a BJP leader.

Vaghela was not amused. Immediately after the elections, he formed the Mahagujarat Asmita Manch. This was a body that would function within the Gujarat BJP and whose first programme was to felicitate Atal Behari Vajpayee who had become prime minister in 1996 (if only for a few days). But it was clear to everyone that this was a body set up as a pressure group within the party. Pandemonium broke out when the Manch held its first programme in mid-March. A 'Khajuria' minister, Atmaram Patel, was manhandled and stripped of his dhoti. In the end, he had to be covered with a party flag. Journalist Deepal Trivedie says: 'His dhoti was torn into shreds. Newspapers of the time reported that Modi was present when Patel was being insulted and that he greatly enjoyed what was happening.' Some journalists were beaten up. 'I remember running into Modi at a hospital where he had come to see a colleague who had got beaten up,' says Sebastian Thomas who was working for the *Times of India* in Ahmedabad. Thomas says that Modi was a frequent visitor to the TOI office 'where he spent hours together chatting with the chief reporter' and 'recognized me as Madrasi bhai'.

In August the same year, by when Deve Gowda was prime minister, Vaghela broke away from the BJP and formed his own party. The BJP state government became unstable and in September, President's Rule was imposed in Gujarat. But this was to be short-lived. Within a month, Vaghela was sworn in chief minister. Needless to add, the government of Vaghela was supported by the Congress. It was also alleged that the governor of the state had played a role in helping the former BJP man ascend to the top post. The government, however lasted only a year, with Vaghela being at the mercy of the Congress which had reduced him to a figurehead. In October 1997, Vaghela resigned, making way for his nominee for the top post. This government, too, only lasted a few months. Elections had to be called in the state. This time, the BJP returned with 117 out of 182 seats in the assembly. Vaghela's party could barely win four seats. Keshubhai became the chief minister and Vaghela, to save his future, had no other option but to join the Congress party.

After being banished to Delhi, Modi rarely came to Gujarat. When he did, his visits were private in nature and he kept away from the RSS headquarters in Ahmedabad or the state BJP office. He began staying in Bopal in the outskirts of Ahmedabad at Sanskardham, a school conceived by Modi's guru, Lakshmanrao Inamdar and started with the help of RSS members.

During Modi's absence, a lot happened in Gujarat. This impacted the Modi government after he took over as chief minister of the state in 2001. When I went to live in Ahmedabad in 2000, I found a city divided and ghettoized. Muslims, however prosperous, were not 'allowed' to own or rent property in the upcoming western suburbs of the city. These were the modern parts to the west of the river Sabarmati in Ahmedabad.

'There was a kind of unwritten code by which no builder would sell houses to Muslims. And no one would rent out their property to a Muslim either. The code was enforced strictly,' says Jamaal Ahmed, a successful architect.

Almost all Muslims in the western part of the city lived in a huge ghetto called Juhapura. Initially a resettlement area for those displaced by severe floods in the river Sabarmati in 1971, Juhapura was originally inhabited by both Hindus and Muslims. But over the years, it became a Muslims-only area. The process of concentration of Muslims intensified after the demolition of the Babri Masjid in 1992.

In Juhapura, civic services were nonexistent and the ghetto even lacked basic infrastructure like branches of banks. A huge wall separated Juhapura from the neighbouring area of Vejalpur. Popularly (but very unfortunately), this was referred to as the Indo-Pakistan border. It is doubtful if any Hindu ever went to Vejalpur. Many people, even those educated and working in good managerial posts, shared in all earnestness, that only 'anti-socials' lived in Juhapura and that they had a cache of arms which they could take up any time.

'What was already a chasm between Hindus and Muslims in the city, grew and became an established way of life in the '90s,' laments Hanif Lakdawala, psychiatrist and social activist. However, in the old city of Ahmedabad, both Muslims and Hindus lived side-by-side. But as in old cities across the country, the residential quarters were divided along caste and religious lines. 'The fact that Muslims cannot aspire to live in middle- and upper-middle-class areas of the new city is a dangerous situation. Such non-engagement between the two communities is fertile ground for communal violence,' a senior police officer shared in 2000.

For his part, Keshubhai did nothing and obviously was not in a position to do anything to reduce the Hindu–Muslim divide. 'The Hindutva elements considered the BJP government to be their own and intensified the process of Hinduization,' says Hanif Lakdawala. For instance, with the mistaken belief that all Hindus are vegetarian, they also insisted that the state become vegetarian. Keshubhai obliged and declared a vegetarian state in Gujarat. Government canteens and Circuit Houses stopped serving non-vegetarian food.

'This often led to a ludicrous situation because places like Junagadh, which was ruled by a Nawab before Independence, had a number of *khansamas* in the Circuit House. While they remained employed with the government, they had no work,' says journalist Rajiv Shah. The vegetarianism was also hypocritical, because Gujarat is a major centre for fishing and government-owned Gujarat Fisheries stalls are to be seen as far north as New Delhi. However, Gujarat Fisheries, through which the state government earned revenues, was allowed to continue to function.

'Except for the upper castes, most Gujaratis have been traditionally non-vegetarian,' says a social scientist. 'So this enforced vegetarianism was obviously an attempt by the Sangh parivar to ramp up upper-caste Hindu values by using the state government,' he adds.

Social mobilization was also pressed into service for this purpose. In 2000, let alone mutton and fish stalls, there were even no eggs to be had in grocery shops in the western suburbs of Ahmedabad.

Hotel buffets consisted of two sections: 'vegetarian' and 'Jain vegetarian' instead of the vegetarian and non-vegetarian that are the norm everywhere else in India.

But Sangh parivar outfits were also mobilizing for a more important purpose: that of spreading the message of Hindutva in the tribal areas of south Gujarat.

These are areas bordering Madhya Pradesh where missionaries had operated for decades and many tribals are Christians. Now, the Sangh parivar wanted to 'Hinduize' them and create captive votes for the BJP. Dangs, the southern-most district of Gujarat bordering Maharashtra with a 90 per cent forest cover and a predominantly tribal population, was chosen. Though many tribes lived here, they had evolved a common Dangi identity in terms of social structure, norms, customs, culture, and language. The Dangis were basically followers of animism, although many of them had become Christians after gaining access to education and health facilities through missionaries. The VHP began celebrations of Hindu festivals like Rama Navami, Hanuman Jayanti, and Krishna Janmasthami in Dangs, drawing the locals into the activities.

After initial success of the programmes they also began to raise battle cries like 'Hindu jago, Christi bhago' and 'galli galli mein shor hai, yeh saab padre chor hai.' Things took a significant turn after Swami Aseemananda, a sadhu from the Sangh parivar outfit Vanvasi Kalyan Parishad, set up shop in Dangs and spread the story that the area was connected to happenings in the Ramayana. Aseemananda claimed that it was here that Rama, in the period of banishment, came across the tribal woman Shabari and accepted a fruit from her. As he bit into the fruit, Shabari was freed from the centuries-old curse she was enduring. Aseemananda set up a temple for Shabari in Dangs and began mobilizing the tribals to worship there. He also began the practice of distributing idols of Hanuman to the tribals. Twenty years later in 2011, Aseemananda was arrested for involvement in the Samjhauta Express, Ajmer and Mecca Masjid blasts. But in Dangs, trouble had first come calling on Christmas Day 1998, when massive riots broke out targeting Christian missionaries and tribals who had converted to Christianity. In interviews, Keshubhai Patel subsequently tried to justify the riots by obliquely stating that missionaries had been misleading the tribals.

4

The Delhi Years

Towards the end of the 1980s, House No 11, Ashoka Road in Lutyen's Delhi, which houses the central party office of the BJP, began buzzing with activity. The Congress party had been in power for the best part of the preceding four decades. But with the Bofors scandal breaking out, public disillusionment had started to set in. Adding to the 'anti-incumbency' wave against the ruling party was the advent of the Ram Temple issue. Many middle-class Indians were in search of an alternative. The BJP which had metamorphosed from its earlier avatar of Jana Sangh via the Janata Party of the post-Emergency days was fast emerging as the answer. Little wonder then that a motley crowd began to visit the national headquarters of the BJP. On their part, the leaders of the BJP were welcoming. For them, the BJP was a fledgling party that required the support of wider sections of citizens. Often, BJP functionaries would hold discussions on subjects of national interest where they invited those whom they perceived to be like-minded individuals who could later be induced into the party. Economists, sociologists, and journalists were on the list of invitees, even though the party faced stiff resistance from some of its members, because a large section of these intellectual classes of India were steeped in socialist and Marxist ideology. A large number of retired bureaucrats also started frequenting 11, Ashoka Road. This group especially included retired officials who felt that they had been given a bad deal by the ruling party and denied promotions despite their capability. Now they wanted to offer their expertise to the new party, bring it to power and thus have their revenge against the Congress.

After the demolition of the Babri Masjid, disgusted by the act of vandalism, many outsiders stopped visiting the BJP office. But with the party's star being on the ascent, other power-seekers who flocked to the BJP headquarters like bees to flowers more than made up for this trend.

'You can say that it was like the Central Hall of Parliament or an animated coffee house, where MPs and others of all shades and colours met to discuss everything under the sun. The only difference was that only folks with a certain type of ideology met. From serious discussion to gossip, everything was part of the game,' says a frequent visitor to the BJP office in those days. Often, what was discussed went a long way in policy-making by the party, and sometimes, even marred or made reputations within the BJP fold.

It was this environment that Narendra Modi stepped into, when he came on deputation to 11, Ashoka Road as a full-time national secretary.

This was going to be his home and office for the next six years.

Modi's arrival evoked mixed reactions. Being on deputation from the RSS, he had his set of admirers, but the circumstances under which he was brought in exile from Gujarat, led to a lot of eyebrows being raised.

'I had known him earlier but I was a little suspicious because of his ways. He did not function the way a full-time RSS pracharak should. He was seen as projecting himself and seeking the limelight,' says a BJP functionary who had his office in 11, Ashoka Road.

The functionary says that his curiosity had been roused by Modi's conduct during the Kanyakumari–Srinagar Ekta Yatra of Murali Manohar Joshi. 'Not only was Modi accompanying Joshiji on his vehicle, but would, at every stop, address the crowds along with the BJP president. As an organizer of the yatra, he should have consciously kept a low profile. It was obvious that he had been able to impress Joshi', he said.

Modi's own set of well-wishers included party men who were opposed to Pramod Mahajan, a rising star in the party at the time. A small-time sub-editor in a Marathi daily till the mid-1980s, Mahajan's RSS background had helped him get close to Advani. In fact, the latter was so impressed by Mahajan that he took him on his Ayodhya Rath Yatra in 1990. Mahajan soon emerged as a top member of Advani's team. This upset Narendra Modi no end, because he had planned at the least the Gujarat leg of the yatra and would not have minded accompanying Advani all the way through himself. However Joshi, who succeeded Advani as BJP president, did give Modi a prime position. But Joshi did not survive too long as the president and soon Advani – and along with him, Pramod Mahajan – was back at the helm. One such Mahajan-baiter then, who witnessed Modi's advent in New Delhi alleges: 'Though Modi was close to Advani, Pramod was closer. Pramod saw a rival in Modi and had him ousted from Gujarat.' This baiter, who is also a BJP leader says: 'Vaghela, who had launched the rebellion in Gujarat, and Pramod were chums. Both were close friends of an industrial group which was known to influence policies in Delhi. They all got together to banish Modi from Gujarat.' Another BJP leader sympathetic to Modi says: 'Narendrabhai was truly a victim of Yatra politics that was plaguing the BJP at that time.'

But whatever Modi's friends may claim, the predominant feeling in the BJP office at that time was that Modi was an upcoming leader who had been given 'too much power by Advani' and who had, in his 'immaturity' exceeded his limits and gone 'overboard' in Gujarat. Hence there was a need to 'cut him down to size', was the opinion.

Despite the bombastic designation, Modi's job as a national secretary meant little. As the in-charge for Himachal Pradesh and under a general secretary of the BJP, Modi was to coordinate the affairs of the state from the party headquarters.

The real challenge for a party functionary is in a state where the party is weak and not in power. In Himachal Pradesh, the party was well organized and had been in power earlier.

In 1995 however, the BJP was not in power in the state. This offered Modi an occasion to go to work. From 1990-1993, the BJP had ruled the state with old party stalwart Shanta Kumar at the helm. But in a subsequent election held two years before Modi arrived in Delhi, the BJP had been routed and the government was run by the Congress.

Even as he started using his networking skills to connect with all BJP office bearers who operated from 11, Ashoka Road and journalists who covered the BJP beat and visited the party office every day, Modi began visiting Shimla.

'I remember Modi since then,' says a senior journalist who is intractably opposed to him. 'But let me tell you, he was unlike Advani and Arun Jaitely who would not even listen to you and start propagating their philosophy. Modi would hear you out before airing his views,' the journalist, who is now an activist, says.

Perhaps Modi in Delhi was careful about what he said, given that those were early days for him yet. Being a RSS pracharak, Modi also leaned heavily on the organization and its core members. 'I remember getting the impression that he was always running around K.S. Sudershan, the sarsanghchalak (overall national boss) of the RSS and cultivating him,' this journalist says.

But a national executive member of BJP differs.

'That was then,' he says. 'Later, Sudershanji was annoyed with Modi's ways and even stopped talking to him.' The national executive member adds: 'Govindacharya, a very important party office bearer, used to treat him with a lot of sympathy then.'

However, one worthy of the Sangh parivar, whom Modi was able to cultivate well, was Dattopant Thengdi, the founder of the Bharatiya Mazdoor Sangh (BMS), the trade union wing of BJP.

This became possible because during his days in Gujarat, Modi had maintained active contact with the BMS unions in the electricity department, state transport corporation, and a few private companies.

After a few visits to Shimla, Modi realized that all was not hunky-dory within the Himachal Pradesh BJP.

There was a new group led by P.K. Dhumal which was interested in sidelining Shanta Kumar, who had lost his seat in the assembly election and had thus become vulnerable. Barely past fifty, Dhumal's ambition had soared after the death of Thakur Jagdev Chand who, along with Shanta Kumar, was one of two most prominent BJP leaders in the state. Soon Dhumal and Modi drew close to each other.

However, the politics of Himachal Pradesh changed due to an unrelated reason: a CBI raid in 1996 at the house of the telecom minister Sukh Ram in Lutyen's Delhi yielded cash of ₹3 crore. Sukh Ram had committed irregularities in awarding telecom contracts. But when found out, he was mightily miffed. Belonging to Himachal Pradesh, he left the Congress party and formed his own Himachal Pradesh Vikas Congress (HVC). This party stood for elections in the Himachal Pradesh assembly elections in 1998 and sealed the fate of the Congress. In a hung assembly – the result of the elections – both Congress and BJP won 31 seats each. Five seats were won by the HVC in the assembly of 68 MLAs and it was clear that Sukh Ram had the casting vote. Not surprisingly, HVC tied up with the BJP and a coalition government came into being in March 1998 with P.K. Dhumal as the chief minister and Sukh Ram as the de facto deputy chief minister who held all the crucial portfolios.

By this time, many had started referring to Modi as Dhumal's mentor. An old-timer remembers how Modi was pressed by newshounds about how the BJP could qualify as a 'party with a difference' (which it advertised itself as), when it thought nothing of tying up with a tainted Sukh Ram against whom CBI had filed criminal complaints (which had been investigated but not acted upon, in the absence of a sanction from the president of India).

Modi was quick to take recourse to mythology and answer: 'In order to usher in Ram Rajya, sometimes you have to take the help of Vibhishana. As narrated in the Ramayana, even Ram had to attack Bali from behind'.

On a more serious note, he said that since the voter had not given a majority to any party, the *janadesh* (people's mandate) message was clear: form a coalition government.

But within a month-and-a-half the state government was rocking again due to the assent from the President of India for the CBI to prosecute Sukh Ram.

For the BJP, it now became untenable to let Sukh Ram continue in the government. No smart answers from Modi would keep tongues from wagging. With Sukh Ram in the government, the image of BJP which prided itself as a party with principles would be seriously dented. Consequently, the party assigned Modi the job of negotiating with Sukh Ram and getting him to step down. This was no easy task as the former telecom minister was unrelenting. But in the end, a reluctant Sukh Ram stepped down and his son entered the Rajya Sabha on the BJP ticket.

In the meantime, winds of change were blowing across the nation. In the 1996 general elections held after the five year reign of Narasimha Rao, the BJP emerged as the largest single party.

At the BJP's annual session in November 1995, L.K. Advani announced that the party's prime ministerial candidate in the general elections slated the following May would be Atal Behari Vajpayee. Since the party had grown in leaps and bounds under the leadership of Advani, the general expectation of the party cadres was that he himself would be projected as the prime minister. But though the BJP's support base had expanded in the preceding ten years, almost all parties treated it as a 'political untouchable.' Given this scenario, Atal Behari Vajpayee was the most acceptable face of the party.

However, even the government headed by Vajpayee collapsed within thirteen days of being sworn in, unable as it was to secure the support of other parties.

In 1998, after fresh elections, Vajpayee was at the helm of the National Democratic Alliance (NDA) government, whose main constituent was the BJP. But this government, too, lasted only thirteen months.

It was not only the external face of BJP that was changing. Internally, too, the BJP was undergoing a metamorphosis. But, there was a contradiction. Though the party projected itself outwardly as a liberal party, it was the reverse among its ranks.

Advani stepped down as the president of the party to be replaced by a full time pracharak, Kushabhau Thakre. An old war-horse, Thakre had been the general secretary in charge of organization from 1993 onwards and was appointed to the top post in 1998. Seventy-six years old when he took office, Thakre had been in the Jana Sangh and BJP since their inception in 1951 and 1980 respectively and in the RSS even longer. He was seen as absolutely loyal to the RSS with a formidable grip over the BJP and its organization. But Thakre was little known and had no clear-cut public image. With the anointment of Thakre, things started looking up for Modi. He was appointed as general secretary of the party along with Govindacharya, Venkaiah Naidu, Sangh Priya Gautam, and Sumitra Mahajan, who was a minister of state in the Vajpayee government. This was Thakre's top team. And yet, the post of general secretary in charge of organization which was earlier held by the new president himself, was still kept vacant. Close watchers averred that this was because Thakre did not want to anoint the most suitable man for the job: Govindacharya. Also, a full-time pracharak on deputation from the RSS and the strategist who had engineered the BJP's extension of its social programme to include backward and other lower castes, Govindacharya was a formidable force.

But Govindacharya had his own set of enemies. Stories about his love for a lady leader of the party started doing the rounds. It was 'Disadvantage Govindacharya' versus 'Advantage Modi'.

In the absence of a full-time general secretary in charge of organization, Thakre had begun to rely upon Modi to handle matters.

Modi's stature was now growing: he was not only being praised for bringing the BJP to power in Himachal Pradesh but also, to an extent, for a fresh BJP victory in Gujarat. Though banished from the state, after he had announced his desire to go to Gujarat and help with elections, his services had been informally requisitioned on the eve of the assembly polls in February 1998.

He was not sent officially because of strong opposition from Sanjay Joshi, the RSS representative who was looking after Gujarat affairs. 'He came to Gujarat and addressed a few meetings. I remember accompanying him to some. In some places he was greeted with cries of 'dekho dekho koun aya, Gujarat ka sher aya'. At others, he was gifted with swords,' says senior journalist Darshan Desai. 'It was clear that despite being banished, Modi still had his organizational men in the state', adds Desai.

The BJP came to power in Gujarat on its own steam. And though the 1998 elections had been managed by Joshi, Modi was able to get part-credit for the victory, by selling the line that the roots of the party in the state had been struck due to his efforts.

'Modi was now being seen as a dedicated general of the BJP, a rising star but nevertheless a hardliner,' says a leader of the BJP who had seen him at close quarters in those days. The party was now also backing him for articulating its views on television. 'He was every inch a hardliner in what he said and his body language on TV shows was very aggressive and a trifle crude,' says a party colleague. 'Many other party leaders were much more refined in the way they spoke.'

But a leading television anchor of that time, Paranjoy Guha Thakurta, says that while Modi might have been aggressive on air, in the waiting room of the studio he was politeness and humbleness personified.

Before the 1998 elections, Modi was made part of the ten-member committee to look after election management and campaigns. In 1999, Thakre also entrusted the job of overseeing party activities in Punjab, Haryana, Jammu & Kashmir, Chandigarh, and Himachal

Pradesh to Modi. The Bharatiya Janata Yuva Manch, the youth wing of the party, too, was placed under Modi's charge.

In 2000, there was another change in the BJP presidency. Bangaru Laxman, a Dalit from Andhra Pradesh, a Vajpayee nominee through-and-through and one devoid of his own base, took over as the new boss. As a representative of a liberal prime minister, he was expected to sideline all hardliners.

But that did not happen. Seen as the hardest liner of the new guard, Govindacharya was dropped from the list of general secretaries to the party.

However, Modi along with Venkaiah Naidu, was retained and even given the crucial charge of organizational matters.

Thus, Modi was now the man responsible for implementing the decisions and programmes of the party. But since the party had expanded rapidly in the preceding years and it would become too unwieldy for one man to handle the charge, he was asked to take the assistance of two vice presidents, Jana Krishnamurthy and Madan Lal Khurana.

At the party headquarters, all roads led to Modi. Since the BJP was in power, favour and position-seekers were making a beeline for government offices from where BJP men presided over ministerial empires.

This is a dilemma that a ruling party always faces. Favour-seekers usually flock to the seat of power and the party attracts people who are prepared to wait for a longer period to make political gains.

A BJP politician, who claims to have been close to Modi at that time, says that in spite of his rapid emergence as a top party leader, Modi was not happy. 'I could discern his frustration. Modi was like a fish out of water in Delhi. His mind was in Gujarat and he wanted to return there. But with Keshubhai as chief minister, nobody really bothered about him back home in Gujarat,' this leader says.

This may have to do with the fact that the party was also changing tack nationally. From being a hard-core saffron party promoting the Ram Temple, the BJP was now trying to push a development agenda.

Modi was probably not in favour of jettisoning the Temple agenda altogether: in fact, party insiders recollect him advising that the post-Babri-Masjid-demolition period should be utilized by the party to consolidate its Hindutva agenda.

But this line of thought was abandoned by the party leadership in light of the post-Babri-Masjid election results. In UP, where Ayodhya is located, the BJP's tally in the 1993 assembly elections (post-Babri demolition) fell significantly from the numbers raked in by the party in the 1991 elections (pre-Babri demolition). Though the Janata Dal and Congress (which were opposed to the Temple agenda) also tumbled, there were gains for the fledgling Bahujan Samaj Party (BSP). The BJP could form a government with the support of that party only by offering the chief minister's post to Mayawati.

Broadly, the same results were repeated in the next assembly election in 1996, confirming that the Ram Temple issue was yielding diminishing results. But in the tribal areas of Gujarat and under the Sangh parivar, the BJP policy of Hindutva was in full force.

As a result, political analysts started describing Gujarat as the 'laboratory of Hindutva.' A BJP leader who worked with Modi in Delhi says: 'In those days Narendrabhai was a strong Hindutva proponent and took up the development plank much later. He was probably yearning to come back to rough and tumble of Hindutva.'

Things changed in Gujarat and also for Modi, on 26 January 2001. A killer earthquake measuring 8.6 on the Richter scale with the epicentre in Kutch had devastating effects across the state.

Although an act of nature, the public mood began to turn away from Keshubhai and the BJP. This had much to do with the fact that relief operations were faulty and delayed. In places like Ahmedabad (located over 400 kilometres from the epicentre of the earthquake) high-rises collapsed leading to a toll of over 750 people. What incensed the public was that these high-rises had been permitted to come up even though the quality of construction was known to be faulty. They began to allege that the contractors and the government were in collusion and that money had changed hands for building permits. 'The public perception was that within barely a few years in power, BJP leaders had begun to emulate the ways of the Congress and become corrupt,' recalls Ashok Patel, an engineer.

'Stories were doing the rounds about how some ruling party netas who used to go around on cycles and two-wheelers had now become owners of big cars. This went a long way in turning the popular mood against the BJP.'

The fact that Keshubhai was seen as lazy, lethargic and surrounded by relatives, too, considerably damaged the image of the ruling BJP.

A few months earlier in 2000, the BJP had lost the municipal elections in Ahmedabad and Rajkot. Ahmedabad was a municipality that it had held since 1987 and Rajkot for over twenty years. The BJP also lost 23 of the 25 districts in the district panchayat elections: a steep decline from the 24 districts that it held before. The defeats were seen as a thumbs-down by the public to the Keshubhai government.

In the weeks after the earthquake, public sentiments on the BJP began to take an even more negative turn. Party bosses in Delhi feared that the results of the municipal elections could well be a precursor to the next assembly elections slated at the beginning of 2003. The party high command turned to Modi – who was present in Delhi – for advice. The advice given by Modi was unequivocal: 'The party was on the path to destruction.'

He also pointed out that the control of the municipalities was the key to power in Gujarat. I remember how Modi had called me on phone around this time to lament how the party that he had set up with toil and hard work was now going to seed. At the BJP's national headquarters, Modi's friends began to float whispers that only someone with strong organizational skills and administrative acumen could pull the party in Gujarat out of the doldrums. Journalist Rajiv Shah remembers how a particular minister in the Keshubhai government used to confidentially brief media persons about what transpired in cabinet meetings immediately after they ended.

'Our understanding was that this briefing was at the behest of someone at the BJP central office in New Delhi,' says Shah. When the information leaked out, it showed up Keshubhai in a bad light. Keshubhai also contributed to his own downfall because of his unskilled public relations and bumbling ways. According to one media report, when asked to inaugurate an 'internet site' by clicking a button, Keshubhai wanted to know how long it would take him by road to reach the site!

After the earthquake, Modi got himself a foothold in Gujarat. As general secretary, he recollects being deputed for relief and rehabilitation work and also constructive party work in the state by the national bosses.

Things came to a head after 20 September, when the BJP lost two by-polls: one to the assembly and the other to the Lok Sabha.

The elections had been slated earlier in the year, but the dislocation in the state administration in the aftermath of the earthquake had resulted in their postponement. The Sabarmati assembly constituency was located right in the heart of Ahmedabad, but it formed a part of the Gandhinagar Lok Sabha seat. The latter seat was held by none other than the party stalwart, L.K. Advani, who had notched up a handsome 45,000 vote lead in the Sabarmati segment of the 1999 elections. Advani was very visible in Ahmedabad those days and therefore the defeat for the BJP in Sabarmati was interpreted as a defeat for Advani. What also alarmed the party was the fact that the people who lived in the constituency were of the lower middle and middle classes and typified the average BJP voter. The Sabarkantha Lok Sabha seat (Sabarkantha is located in north Gujarat), had a significant chunk of tribal voters whom the party had successfully wooed in previous years. The Congress candidate in the elections, Madhusudhan Mistry, was a close associate of Shankersinh Vaghela but came from an NGO background. Though the seat had fallen vacant due to the death of the sitting Congress MP Nisha Amarsinh Chaudhary, the BJP went all out to wrest it. In fact, some BJP campaigners harped on the '*krishti–non kristhi*' (Christian–non Christian) angle, suggesting that the Congress party was an outfit of Christians not only because 'foreigner' Sonia was at the helm, but also because Mistry ran NGOs who received foreign funding. Mistry's flowing, white hair, too lent him the aura and appellation of a missionary.

But for the BJP, all this was in vain.

By now, the BJP bosses in Delhi were convinced that Keshubhai had to be replaced. Word leaked out and daily delegations of aspirants and their associates shuttled between Ahmedabad and Delhi, offering their candidature or lobbying for their candidates. But Keshubhai was in no mood to step down. He was aware the party's main support base consisted of Patels and that he was their undisputed leader. 'Therefore he thought that it was not right for anyone to ask for his head. Keshubhai, of course did not realize that his indifferent administrative skills and bad communication abilities were doing him in,' says an IAS officer who served in Keshubhai's government in an important position. 'Keshubhai also believed that he was implementing the Sangh parivar agenda very well and that therefore, it could only be somebody with a personal grudge who wanted him removed,' says another civil servant who worked with Keshubhai. To save his job and position, Keshubhai organized the signatures of 30 MLAs who were his hardcore supporters and sent them to Delhi. When this strategy did not work, Keshubhai forwarded his choice for new chief minister. This was Vallabh Kathiria, an MP who was also a minister of state in the Vajpayee government. The low-profile Kathiria was a physician, a Patel, and a staunch loyalist of Keshubhai. But the party high command had already made up its mind on sending Modi for the top job in Gandhinagar, though there was severe in-house jostling with new BJP president Jana Krishnamurthy, party vice-president in-charge of Gujarat, Madan Lal Khurana, and Kushabhau Thakre getting into the fray. For public consumption, the party spokesmen flatly denied that any change was being contemplated but later on insisted that nothing was 'final'. When a journalist questioned Prime Minister Vajpayee, all that he was willing to say was that yes, the by-election results were an indicator that it was a '*chunauti ki ghadi*', adding however that whatever decision would be taken would be with '*sarvasammati*' (on the basis of a consensus). I remember a journey from Delhi to Ahmedabad on an evening flight in the last week of September, when I encountered dozens of Gujarat politicians returning back home. Among them was Haren Pandya, home and information minister in the Keshubhai government. Appearing a little crestfallen, he told me: 'It appears that it will be Modi.' Obviously, Haren was wary of Modi.

On 2 October, Keshubhai was called to Delhi and told in no uncertain terms that he would have to step down and was forced to give a resignation letter to the party president Jana Krishnamurthy. A sullen Keshubhai came back to Ahmedabad the same evening and said that nobody had asked him to quit as yet. In any case, the legislature party would have to meet to choose its leader. Meanwhile, his finance minister Suresh Mehta, who had been chief minister earlier, pointed out that since Modi was not even a MLA, he would be unacceptable as a new chief minister. But a day later and after Keshubhai was steam-rolled into submitting his resignation, the way was paved for Modi.

At a meeting of BJP MLAs, Keshubhai was persuaded by the high command to propose Modi's name and Suresh Mehta to second it.

Thus, Modi was 'unanimously' elected as the BJP legislative party chief. On 7 October 2001, he was sworn in as chief minister.

Commenting on the manner in which Keshubhai was removed and Modi installed, a Sangh parivar insider says: 'By this time the BJP in power at the Centre had started behaving exactly the way the Congress party had done during its rule. The high command had become supreme and there was no effort to figure out whether it was Keshubhai or Modi, who had the majority of MLAs behind him.'

Though most political watchers felt that Modi had lobbied intensely to secure the job, Sangh parivar-watcher Arvind Bosmia avers that Modi was chosen not because he was a favourite of the high command but because 'he was not seen as one who would command a majority on his own.'

Bosmia adds: 'Modi was known to be brash and the high command felt that he would have to depend heavily on the support of the bosses in Delhi to run the government. Hence his selection.'

But this was a gross miscalculation. Little did the party leaders realize that they were unleashing a chief minister who would, within just a year, become so powerful that he would care for just about nobody within the party.

'The signs were there for discerning eyes but nobody noticed,' says Darshan Desai. 'For instance, I remember the opening line of a story in a newspaper: "Move over Atal, Modi is here". The story was prompted by the response that Modi was attracting at public meetings after the earthquake. It was greater than what Vajpayee would have attracted.'

શાળાની જુ. ડિ. એન.સી.સી.ની એક ટ્રૂપ

Modi as part of his school's junior division NCC Troupe. (Modi not correctly identifiable but perhaps sitting first from right in the second row.)

Narendra Modi, along with former Gujarat chief minister Keshubhai Patel, taking a salute with the top brass of the right-wing Hindutva outfit Rashtriya Swayamsevak Sangh (RSS) at a meeting. This was before he fell out with them.

Modi, with senior BJP leader L.K. Advani, flashes the victory sign in Ahmedabad after BJP's third consecutive landslide victory in the Gujarat Assembly elections. A larger than life poster of his looks on (December 2012).

Narendra Modi supporters, wearing Modi masks, rejoice in the wake of his third election win.

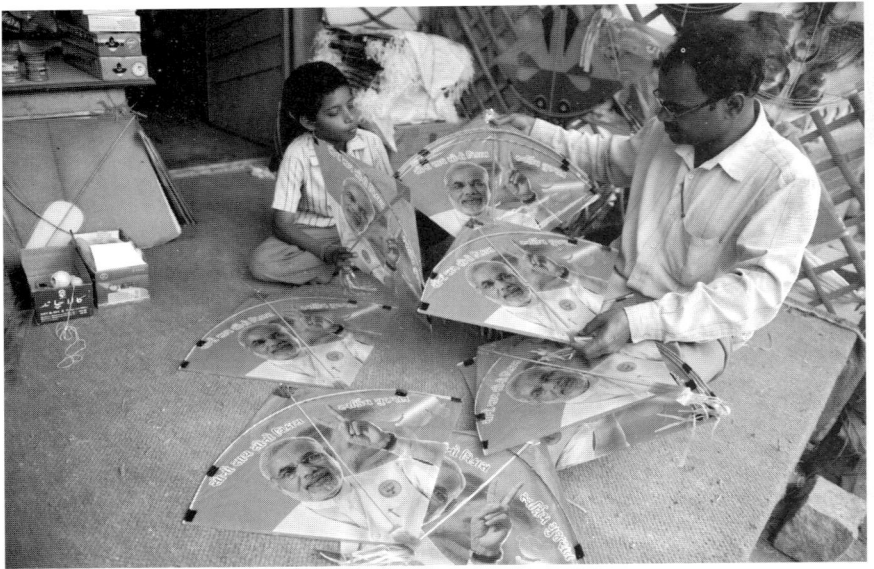

A kite vendor shows off his stock of kites bearing Narendra Modi's pictures.

Narendra Modi's mother offers him sweets during his visit following his third straight victory in the Gujarat Assembly Elections in December 2012.

Modi hugs the Reliance Industries Ltd. chairman, Mukesh Ambani, at the Vibrant Gujarat 2013 Summit in Gandhinagar.

Modi waves to the gathering at the inauguration of the Vibrant Gujarat 2013 Summit, as the Japanese ambassador to India Takeshi Yagi (left), and Canadian High Commissioner Stewart Beck (right) look on.

Modi, with the then Tata group chairman Ratan Tata, at the announcement of the shifting of the Tata Nano plant from Singur in West Bengal to Sanand on the outskirts of Ahmedabad (October 2008).

Modi armed with a camera, atop a hot air balloon, looking down on the newly revamped Kankaria Lakefront.

Modi with senior BJP leader and former prime minister, Atal Behari Vajpayee.

5

Riots and After

On the eve of his swearing-in on 6 October 2001, accompanied by the state BJP chief, Rajendrasinh Rana and home and information minister (in the outgoing Keshubhai regime), Haren Pandya, Narendra Modi, the designate-chief minister visited newspaper offices in Ahmedabad. The incumbent chief minister's tone was one of solicitation and appeal: please help me in running the state, let us work together to make Gujarat great. Modi touched base not only with editors, but made it a point to interact with reporters and other staff too. While the journalists were floored by this gesture, the faces of Modi's companions were expressionless. It appeared as though the duo had been dragged along on a burdensome expedition against their wishes.

The visit to the newspaper offices was among the first of trips undertaken by Modi during the last three days of his camping out in Suite 1A of the Circuit House in Gandhinagar, about 30 kilometre from Ahmedabad. Modi was having long marathon meetings in the suite from 9 am till late in the night. Rarely did he leave the room, other than to meet with large groups of people who came to greet him and could not be accommodated in the suite. But no matter how late he called it a day, Modi was up at 5 am. One of the first things he then asked for was newspapers. For the staff at the Circuit House, this was proving to be a problem because the dailies were not delivered before 8:30 am. But Modi was insistent: if there were no newspapers, could he, at least, have downloads of the internet editions, the new boss asked. The staff were even more flummoxed: used to the slothful culture of sarkari offices in the state capital, they were usually asked to deliver tea and tasty snacks in the morning, not newspapers. Nobody had made such demands on them before.

By 9 am, bureaucrats were called in and meetings would begin in earnest. 'We realized that we were in a new regime. Work would be conducted in a new fashion, with a lot of orientation on information collection and dissemination,' says IAS officer S.K. Nanda, who served as secretary to the Government of Gujarat in those days. 'Modi told us that the government cannot deliver all services and we should increasingly rope in non-governmental organizations to improve efficiency,' Nanda recollects.

Modi had his spiel ready and was saying different things to different target groups. To party-men, Modi was emphasizing the need for internal unity and to keep their counsel to themselves. 'Keep away from characters like Manthara. They are worse than Ravan,' Modi told visitors. 'Internal enemies who constantly poison the minds of colleagues are worse than external foes that can be effectively dealt with,' Modi said. (Manthara is the maid of Rama's step mother Kaikeyi in the epic Ramayana. It is on Manthara's prompting that Kaikeyi tricks her husband Dasaratha to banish Rama to the forests.)

The prodigal son of Gujarat had returned home. Notwithstanding the great energy he was displaying, Modi's induction was not smooth. The list of ministers who would be sworn in along with Modi could only be finalized at 1 am on the eve of the swearing in, what with constant pulls and pressures. Keshubhai had exited but he wanted some of his key-men accommodated. Then there was the need to keep former chief minister Suresh Mehta, who had aligned with Keshubhai and was a Vajpayee man, happy too. In the end and in what was largely a compromise, Modi was sworn in along with nine ministers. But the function at which he was administered the oath of office was glittering, to say the least.

Away from Raj Bhavan, Modi's swearing-in was at the helipad in Gandhinagar, on a 1800 square feet special podium set up below a 23 feet dome that had been erected specially for the occasion. Large crowds thronged this one lakh square-foot covered area and many of Modi's political friends from his non-VIP days at New Delhi made a beeline for it too. For them, Modi offered inspiration: how any of them working in the BJP central office, too, could make it to the top post.

The coming days for Modi were a constant reminder of the tough battle that he would have to wage to survive. Though not an MLA, he had been appointed chief minister of Gujarat by the high command. But neither his partymen, nor the oppositional Congress nor the general public, were ready to give him full support. For starters, he needed an assembly seat from where he could contest: after all he had never been in electoral politics before and never held a public post. Nobody was rushing in to oblige him. As per the constitutional mandates, he had only six months to find a seat and get elected to the legislative assembly. Word began to leak that Modi was eyeing the Ellisbridge assembly constituency located in the heart of urban Ahmedabad. It had a sizeable number of voters who were inclined to the BJP, but the problem was that Haren Pandya held that seat. He was in no mood to oblige Modi and had conveyed this quite bluntly to the new chief minister. Ultimately, Modi had to zero in on a seat in Rajkot which was in the heartland of Keshubhai and managed to get the seat vacated by prompting Vajubhai Vala, finance minister in the former government against whom there were many corruption charges. Vala was in the construction business and had drawn flak post the earthquake. Charges had been levelled against him by Modi too.

Rajkot was located in the heart of Saurashtra and had earlier been the cultural capital of Gujarat. Even though groundnut was raised here, water supply was scarce. The situation was so bad that water was supplied only for four days in a month by the Rajkot municipality. It was customary for office staffers to ask their employers for a monthly 'water allowance' as part of their wages to buy water in the flourishing black market. But Rajkot had a very politically-conscious electorate and to satiate their demand for news, the city had not only morning dailies but flourishing evening papers too. Modi arrived for the Rajkot II seat, seeking votes and – making promises like all politicians do: 'I shall ensure that you get supply of water for 22 days against the 4 days now. I will deliver Narmada water here.' The local vested interests controlled by the *telia rajas* (the groundnut cartel) – responded in the way they knew best: by increasing the black market in edible oil and sending their prices up. 'This is all political. They are taking advantage of the situation,' Modi said. 'I am an honest man, vote for me. I cannot be dishonest. I don't have family to look after.'

On 24 February 2002, though Vajubhai Vala had won the seat by more than double the number when he was elected, Modi was returned with a fairly large majority of over 14,000 votes. To observers, the BJP was clearly on the down slide in Gujarat. As if to buttress the trend, the BJP lost two other assembly seats to which elections had been held along with that of Rajkot. Both the seats were won by the Congress, one wrested from the BJP. Political pundits were projecting that the BJP and Modi would be ousted in the next assembly elections in the beginning of 2003. But the world was to change in precisely three days.

When something becomes a matter of faith, truth becomes the casualty. Whatsoever the burden of evidence, people will believe what they want to. Belief is so unshakeable, that even evidence to the contrary will not shake it.

The only thing certain about the Godhra train incident is that on 27 February 2002, the sleeper coach S6 of the Ahmedabad-bound Sabarmati Express was burnt down. Fifty-nine passengers perished in the fire, most of them *kar sevaks* returning from Ayodhya. The train had originated in Lucknow and most of the *kar sevaks* had boarded the reserved compartments without reservations. The journey was marred by continual disturbances. Reports suggest that batches of *kar sevaks* had been returning by trains every day during the previous week, getting down at various railway stations and squabbling with vendors, including at Godhra. Whether the fire was set off deliberately by the Muslim residents of Signal Falia, the area adjoining Godhra railway station as a result of a planned conspiracy, or, whether the coach went up in flames after an altercation on platform number 1 of the station at around 7.45 am that fateful morning, will perpetually remain a matter of conjecture with no consensus on how events unfolded.

After an altercation on the platform (as a result of provocation and counter provocation: it is suggested that perhaps a *kar sevak* tugged at the beard of a Muslim vendor, or an attempt was made to molest a young girl waiting at the platform), massive stoning began. This was even as the train started moving forward and the passengers inside the train began downing their window-shutters to escape the stones. However, after a few hundred metres, somebody pulled the emergency chain and the train came to a halt. Then it started once but – halted again. At this point, a fire broke out. A survivor of the carnage – who was on the fateful S6 sleeper coach – was unable to say precisely how it did. He said that during the heavy stoning, he had hidden under the seat. When the fire broke out, he had crawled towards the door on the other side – away from where the stones were being thrown – and made his escape. The doors at the end from where the stones were thrown had been latched from outside by the stone throwers.

However, for the record, a special court has tried the Godhra conspiracy case and convicted 31 Muslims. The court upheld the case of the prosecution that the incident was a result of pre-planned conspiracy. However, it absolved and let off the prime conspirator, Haji Umarji. A total of 63 accused were acquitted in the case. The judge held that bogey S6 was first locked from the outside to prevent those inside from escaping. After this, the vestibules were opened, petrol flung inside, and the coach set on fire. According to the prosecution, the conspiracy to burn the sleeper coach had been hatched the previous night at a guest house close to the railway station. But the point to be noted is that the train, which was scheduled to reach Godhra in the wee hours of night, was many hours late that morning.

Though the court upheld the case made by the prosecution that had been earlier investigated by the Gujarat police, the initial assessment of the police had been different from what was ultimately presented in court.

Standing on the Godhra platform exactly a month after the incident, the then chief investigations officer, K.C. Bawa and a special inspector general of police, P.P. Agja, shared that if there was a conspiracy behind the incident, then they were yet to find evidence of it. When queried how the train could have burnt down, Agja said that he did not know, but that hypothetically, it could have resulted from an altercation between the *kar sevaks* and the large number of Muslim tea sellers at the station. The hawkers carried stoves, so setting something on fire was not impossible. Further, the seats in the train had rexin covers that could catch fire easily.

Agja also remarked that the residents of Signal Falia were known for their unruly ways. Many other police officers that I spoke to, seemed to agree. Soon after Agja's views were carried in the TOI, he was transferred out and Bawa retired. A new team was set up. The Justice U.C. Banerjee Commission of enquiry set up by Railway Minister Laloo Prasad Yadav in 2004, also came to the conclusion that the fire was accidental and not a result of inflammable liquid thrown from outside but due to presence of some combustible stuff inside the train itself.

On the evening of 27 February when the gory incident took place, entertainment-starved Ahmedabad was enraptured by a cultural performance.

Even as the Sabarmati Express with its remaining passengers on board slowly chugged into Vadodara and Ahmedabad, the upper echelons of society were at the Karnavati Club, listening to Jagjit Singh ghazals.

If there was disquiet about the gory incidents of the morning, there were no signs of it. At the open-air show, the audience enjoyed the music, frequently strolling up to food stalls to pick up snacks. In fact, Jagjit Singh was disturbed by the audience walking up and down and at one point threatened to stop singing.

But by the next morning, the city was up in flames. Marauding mobs went around with trishuls, petrol and whatever they could lay their hands on to indulge in arson and destruction. The Vishwa Hindu Parishad had called for a Gujarat bandh on the day (followed by a Bharat bandh the day after), but the roads were teeming with murderous crowds. The targets, of course, were Muslim localities and Muslim business establishments. In affluent areas, even the well-to-do came out to ransack business establishments. In this mayhem, if there was anyone who was conspicuous by their absence, it was the police. For some strange reason, even the entire traffic police force of Ahmedabad, Gujarat's main city, was missing. The carnage was not limited to Ahmedabad but spread to Vadodara (110 kilometre away). In rural areas in central Gujarat, hundreds of hapless Muslims were killed, unprotected by the police against the mass fury. In many places, marauding mobs were led by local politicians. For the first time, trouble broke out in tribal areas of Gujarat too. However, south Gujarat (which has the major city of Surat) and Saurashtra (except for Bhavnagar) were unaffected by the trouble.

Some of the most gruesome incidents took place in Ahmedabad city. In Naroda Patiya, 97 Muslims including women and children, were killed. In a locality inhabited by Muslims, a mob of 5000 attacked the Noorani Masjid and set it on fire by blasting LPG cylinders. What followed was ten hours of mayhem that saw the Muslims being chased into pits that were then set on fire. In the midst of this, there were rapes and sexual assaults. Naroda Patiya was populated by 2000 Muslims from Maharashtra and Karnataka, who were daily wage labourers. The marauders were led by a VHP worker, Babu Bajrangi, who, rather perversely, saw himself as a social reformer. The local BJP MLA Maya Kodnani, who subsequently became a minister, was also at hand, leading the crowds. The police stood passively and looked the other way. If their duty was to maintain law and order, then this was something that they were oblivious to on the crucial day. In Gulberg Society of Memaninagar, not too far away, a housing society was burnt down and 70 people, including a former MP who represented Ahmedabad earlier in the Lok Sabha, were killed. Huge murderous crowds had been gathering outside the society since the morning even as the former MP, Ehsan Jafri made phone calls to powerful people asking for help. The police failed to provide adequate protection. The incident happened after the local additional commissioner of police visited the place in the afternoon and his departure was taken as the signal by the waiting crowds that the police would not intervene or come back to help.

Mobs scaled the walls of the gated community, threw stones and bulbs filled with acid. They also blasted LPG cylinders. It was a particularly gruesome incident because the former MP was first beaten up, and then stripped. Then his body parts were chopped off and finally he was burnt. The story of what happened in Gulberg Society was later made into a sensitive Hindi movie, *Parzania*, directed by Gujarati filmmaker, Rahul Dholakia.

Similar incidents were playing out in Vadodara where the well-known Best Bakery Case took place. A bakery owned by a Muslim was burnt down along with 14 people, of whom 12 were Muslims. Even as the police were inert, two ministers of the Modi ministry – Ashok Bhatt and I.K. Jadeja – were stationed at the headquarters of the police communication centre, for reasons yet unclear. I remember calling Ashok Bhatt expressing concern about the mayhem. He did not react and did not tell me that he was sitting at the police control room. Smoke billowed over the city but the mayhem did not stop at the end of the first day.

On the night of 28 February, a mob stormed the Dipda Darwaja areas of Visnagar town of Mehsana district, not far from Ahmedabad, and killed 11 members of a Muslim family, including women and children. In Sardarpura of the same district, 33 Muslims were burnt alive by a mob. In Ode town of Anand district, a 2000-strong mob gathered near Pirawali Bhagol and on 1 March, mobs set fire to a house where Muslim women and children had taken shelter. Twenty-three were killed. Gang-rape cases were reported, one of the most notorious being that of Bilkis Bano. The young woman, who was fleeing her village on 3 March to escape the wrath of mobs, was gang raped even as her three-year-old daughter was clobbered to death. Fourteen members of her family were also killed. The rapists and killers were all known to her: in fact, her husband supplied milk to them every morning.

In tribal areas, mobs raided shops and establishments owned by Muslims. Many of the Muslims – from the Bohra community – were also money lenders: the tribals destroyed the documents relating to loans that they had taken from them. There were reports that in places, instead of helping victims, the police were joining the marauders. A senior police officer lamented how, in many instances when Hindu mobs came face-to-face with Muslims, the police fired on the latter. Reports of mobs pursuing injured Muslims even inside hospitals, also came to light. Though the riots targeted Muslims, a senior Gujarat police official, R.B. Sreekumar, later found out that 66 per cent of all those killed in police firing comprised of Muslims. If the Muslims were at the receiving end, police firing should have been directed at the Hindu marauding forces. But what happened was the reverse.

The law of the jungle prevailed: it provoked more lawlessness and led to more mindless acts. Outside the office of the police commissioner of Ahmedabad and on the edge of the main road was the mazaar of famous Urdu poet, Vali Dakhni (an inspiration for later-day poets Mir Taqi Mir and Mirza Ghalib) who, in the seventeenth century, had migrated to the city from the Deccan and had penned many immortal verses in praise of Gujarat. He loved Gujarat so much that his name had been changed to Vali Gujarati.

Vali Gujarati's mazaar was vandalized. Instead of reconstructing the grave, civic officials quickly removed all traces of the mazaar and paved and extended the road over it.

There was virtually no voice of sanity. Even those who did not participate in the mayhem themselves, egged on aggressors by giving them moral support.

It was as if the entire Gujarati society held the community of Gujarati Muslims responsible for the Godhra train incident, even though it had taken place far from Ahmedabad. The collective national conscience was jolted by these acts and yet, the local press seemed in synch with the mood in the state. Worse still, representatives of the Congress party who should have been galvanized into action, because the trouble-makers were supposed to have links with the Sangh parivar, were untraceable. Gujarat Pradesh Congress chief and former chief minister, Amarsinh Chaudhary, was nowhere to be seen. Protesting the mayhem were only members of NGOs but their voices did not carry far. In some places though, local communities refused to be drawn into the rioting: a good example is a 20,000-populated slum, Ram Rahim Nagar, that had both Hindus and Muslims living side-by-side, which maintained absolute peace. In many places, Dalits who had lived cheek-by-jowl with Muslims, were being drawn into the conflict for the first time. Leaders of the Left and the Samajwadi Party did arrive in town on the night of 28 February, but they were unable to get the police commissioner to act.

News of the trouble shook the Delhi establishment. Defence Minister George Fernandes was dispatched to Ahmedabad to deploy the army (if the state government wanted it) and bring the situation under control. Fernandes, a socialist who had visited Ahmedabad in

1969 as an activist in the midst of major riots, was shocked by what he saw. I met him on 2 March at the Circuit House in Ahmedabad. Though I had no previous acquaintance with Fernandes, the minister sent away the chief secretary and other heads of civil administration, and sought a detailed report from me. It was clear from the conversation that Fernandes was getting contra-indications about the intention and seriousness of the government in trying to put down the violence. At the end of a three-hour conversation, Fernandes volunteered that he had heard that the arsonists had been given three days to do whatever they wanted. I told him that this was unconfirmed news off the grapevine. The meeting ended when minister of state for defense, Harin Pathak – who was also the Ahmedabad MP and hardcore Hindutva man, – barged into the room. He flung himself on the sofa: his body language suggesting that he did not want this meeting to continue.

Meanwhile, Modi was seen doing nothing to control the situation. There were murmurs in the senior echelons of the police that their chief had been asked to keep silent. There were stories doing the rounds about how Narendra Modi had called a meeting of senior civil and police officials at his home on the evening of 27 February saying that if there was a Hindu reaction it should be 'allowed.' The allegation of such a statement being made by Modi has persisted for many years. But it has been denied by Modi, who was many years later quizzed by officials of the Special Investigation Team (SIT) appointed by the Supreme Court.

The SIT gave him a clean chit by saying that there was no 'prosecutable evidence' to try Modi.

Of course, the fact that such a meeting to review law and order was held, has never been denied.

I asked Narendra Modi's then private secretary, Anil Mukim, whether his boss had ever spoken of allowing a 'Hindu reaction'. He told me: 'Not in my presence.' However, it is a fact that the decision to bring the bodies of those who perished in the Godhra train carnage to Ahmedabad was taken at a meeting presided over by Modi, even though civil servants and police had warned that such a move was ill-advised and could lead to a law-and-order situation. The charred bodies were brought in trucks to Ahmedabad in the wee hours of the morning of 28 February. This contributed towards inflaming the public mood, especially because no curfew had been imposed in anticipation of trouble. It was also strange that the bodies of those killed in Godhra were handed over to the office bearers of the VHP, and not to the next-of-kin of the deceased, as established procedures require.

Rioting started in the early morning of 28 February. In one of the first instances, a British Gujarati Muslim family returning to their ancestral village, was way laid on the highway and killed. Modi's minister Haren Pandya, who was later slain, told me that he had also advised against a move to bring the bodies to Ahmedabad, but was shouted down by cabinet colleagues who said that a 'reaction' in Ahmedabad would benefit the BJP in the next elections.

Pandya subsequently tendered this evidence in camera to a Citizens' Tribunal comprising retired high court judges. He told them about a meeting of ministers where Modi had talked about allowing a 'Hindu reaction'.

I later asked Pandya whether he had, in fact, given such a testimony and what made him do so. He claimed that he understood the 'Hindu anger' as a reaction to the Godhra incident but could not reconcile with the killing of people in retaliation.

Incidentally, Pandya was also part of a mob which had participated in arson, but not killings. An inquiry by the National Human Rights Commission later reported that the then home minister, Gordhan Zadaphia, had raised his fingers in a victory signal even as the killings were going on in Ahmedabad. So bad were the riots, that even a sitting Muslim judge of the Gujarat high court was targeted at his official residence. He had to be rescued by well-wishers and shifted elsewhere. The collector of Gandhinagar – a Muslim – had his car stoned by protestors. In many parts of the state, hoardings came up welcoming visitors to the 'Hindu rashtra'. For instance, a sign at a location in Ahmedabad welcomed them to the 'Karnavati city of Hindu rashtra' (Karnavati is the ancient Hindu name of the place where Ahmedabad came up in 1411). When Sheela Bhatt, a journalist queried the president of the VHP, Keka Shastri, as to how marauding crowds were able to target commercial establishments owned by Muslims — in spite of their carrying no board proclaiming their ownership — and leave out Hindu-owned establishments, he said that a list of the ownership of establishments — religion-wise — was available with his organization.

Though the intensity of the one-sided riots abated after some days, they continued for months till decorated police officer, K.P.S. Gill was appointed security advisor to the Gujarat government in May.

Gill activated the police in Ahmedabad and gave marching orders to the police commissioner P.C. Pande who had been inert from day one.

Pande was later rewarded and a few years later, Modi promoted him as the director-general of police, a position from which he retired.

Gill famously remarked how he was disturbed by the absence of the 'Kalinga effect' in Gujarat, an allusion to the remorse felt by Emperor Ashok after he had killed thousands in the battlefields of Kalinga. There are no exact numbers of those killed in the riots; estimates vary between 1000 and 2000. However, official records claim that 1267 persons were killed, of whom more than 70 per cent were Muslims. The variance in the figures occurs because many bodies were not found or, were given mass burials. The saffron brigade argues that it was not a one-sided riot because Hindus were killed in the police firing too. This is not incorrect and really happened — ironically — in those places where local police followed the law of the land and acted as they should.

In Surat for instance, no riots erupted on 28 February because the local commissioner of police, Vineet Gupta, firmly maintained law and order. The real problem was in Ahmedabad where the commissioner, P.C. Pande, abdicated his duties. Even the top police chief, K. Chakravarthi, could not muster enough courage to stand his ground and insist his officers follow the police manual strictly. However, his close colleagues of the time note that he was unhappy and repeatedly expressed his disillusionment. Many younger police officers like Rahul Sharma, the SP of Bhavnagar, acted as per their conscience and refused to heed the instructions of the district collector and raid a Madarsa where fugitive Muslims had taken refuge. He was transferred out. But on a later assignment – considered a 'side-lined' post – and for the purpose of investigation, he was able to gather cell-call details of many top ministers and political executives on the crucial day of 28 February.

In the interim and very conveniently, these records have been 'lost' by the Gujarat government.

In many incidents, the FIRs filed by the police were flawed. They were drafted so as to make it impossible to convict anyone. In the Best Bakery case, the FIR was filed in such a way that it gave the impression that those killed had brought on trouble upon themselves. Although the draconian provision of the Prevention of Terrorism Act (POTA) had been invoked in the case of those accused and arrested in the Godhra case, the Act was not used to charge the post-Godhra riot aggressors. Furthermore and in many cases, VHP functionaries were appointed as public prosecutors.

Incidents – some revolting – of significant import continued for months together: like the case of a Hindu woman who was riding pillion on a two-wheeler driven by her Muslim husband. Marauders yanked her off the scooter, stripped her and knifed her to death. They then left the naked body on the road in Ahmedabad city and went away.

Having witnessed the riots closely, I can say with authority that any government that showed such indifference in controlling the carnage elsewhere in the country would have been dismissed immediately and the state put under President's Rule. But Modi's godfather, L.K. Advani was the home minister. While he steadfastly protected Modi, other Modi well-wishers, like Arun Jaitely, argued in Delhi that the liberal press in Gujarat was 'hyping' the situation and misreporting. The then BJP president, Jana Krishnamurthy and RSS leader, Kushabhau Thakre also lobbied for Modi within the organization. Even as international condemnation mounted thick and fast, President K.R. Narayanan wrote to Prime Minister Atal Behari Vajpayee, expressing his concern. On 4 April, disturbed by the reports, Vajpayee arrived in Gujarat. He advised Modi to follow 'rajdharma' only to receive an angry riposte from the chief minister on live television that he was, indeed, doing so. Organizations like Human Rights Watch (HRW) documented the horrors of post-Godhra violence. Appropriately, the HRW report was titled: 'We have no orders to save you'. The allusion was to the police response to Muslims seeking help. A team of the Editors Guild of India, too, compiled a report on the 'horrors' of the riot and noted the 'supine, if not complicit behaviour of the state.'

The Gujarat government's efforts at relief and rehabilitation were half-hearted.

Within a month of the riots, more than 100,000 displaced persons had moved into 101 relief camps. Within a few weeks, that number swelled to 150,000. These relief camps were set up by NGOs and community groups that had rushed to Gujarat from all over the country. Meanwhile, the Gujarat government tried to close down the camps, because they gave the state a bad name. It also refused to set up more relief camps, declaring that there was no guarantee that the people who were camped there were not carrying arms for retaliation.

All through this period, Modi's popularity was rising in Gujarat; even the educated classes were enamoured by him. Modi was successfully employing the slogan 'Gujarati Asmita' (the pride of Gujarat) to captivate his audience and blunt external condemnation.

I remember two instances when I was given a dressing-down for 'unfairly portraying' the state of affairs in Gujarat. The first time, I was called in by a group of intellectuals that included a professor of IIM Ahmedabad and other academics. The second time, a subtler message came from a group of leading industrialists. They said that the reports carried by the national press were damaging investment prospects in Gujarat.

On another occasion, VHP secretary Praveen Togadia organized to meet me at the house of a common acquaintance and threatened that I would be socially boycotted, if I did not 'mend my ways.'

'No servant will work at your house, no shopkeeper will sell their wares to your wife,' Togadia threatened. During the long rioting, I had occasion to meet Modi a couple of times. In private, Modi pleaded helplessness and said that he was trying to do his best. '*Apko pata nahin Musalmanon ke liye merey dil mein kitna dard hai*,' he told me, thumping his chest. But these private statements did not tally with his public responses. I also remember how angry he was with police officer Rahul Sharma who had refused to raid a Madarsa, 'for trying to seek cheap publicity and act like a hero.' Modi was never seen coming out in public to campaign for peace. His movements suggested the contrary. Though he had visited Godhra and consoled victims of the carnage, he failed to visit the sites of other massacres like Naroda Patiya and Gulberg Society immediately. Perhaps he was too scared to face the relatives of the victims.

In spite of this support in his home state, an agitated Vajpayee, himself under attack for persisting with Modi, ultimately decided to get rid of the chief minister. On 11 April, I received a phone call from the close aide of the then governor, Sundar Singh Bhandari to tell me that Arun Jaitely, the law minister at the time, was flying in from Delhi to secure Modi's resignation and that it would be announced at the national executive meeting of the BJP slated in Goa the next day.

But Modi pulled off a coup. At the Goa meeting, second-rung leaders of the BJP came out in strong support of Modi. Vajpayee was left red-faced and, to salvage the situation, turned strident himself. A BJP insider says: 'I asked Vajpayeeji, who, after all, had decided that Modi should go, as to why he finally acquiesced to Modi's continuance'.

Vajpayee told the insider, that on the flight to Goa, he had been 'put under immense pressure by party functionaries and had to give in.'

At that time, the only way Modi could have been removed was if the main allies of the BJP in the National Democratic Alliance – Janata Dal (U), TDP, and DMK had forced the matter. But the parties decided against it because they thought that the pressure building up for Modi was so strong, that the union government would collapse. People like Chandrababu Naidu and Nitish Kumar, though not comfortable with what was going on, were more interested in retaining power.

Emboldened by his new lease of life, Modi wanted to dissolve the assembly prematurely and go for elections. But members of the Election Commission of India, led by Chief Election Commissioner J.M. Lyngdoh, visited Gujarat and received reports that the atmosphere was not conducive for elections. The open-house testimony to the commission advising against polls, came from R.B. Sreekumar, additional director general of Intelligence. Sreekumar was later jettisoned from his post and denied promotion. He got his promotion to the rank of director-general of police only after he retired, with orders from the court. Though he could not serve as director general, he received the benefit of a higher pension due to the court order.

There was an attempt to socially ostracize Sreekumar: many of his colleagues in office who lived in the same apartment complex as he did, advised him to fall in line. But Sreekumar did not relent and testified before a Gujarat government-established enquiry commission. He told the commission that there was 'pervasive subversion of government machinery to sabotage justice delivery to riot victims and this has to be understood as a man-made disaster, caused by a lack of integrity and professionalism from the chief minister down to the constables.'

Modi was upset that the Lyngdoh-led Election Commission refused to hold elections before November, on the grounds that conditions had not returned to normal and that it was not possible to revise the electoral rolls. The Election Commission made a reference to the Supreme Court and the latter agreed. Meanwhile, Modi publicly mocked the Election Commissioner, referring to his Christian origin and therewith his supposed closeness to another Christian, Sonia Gandhi, as the reason for 'biased' action. He said that all this was 'sochi samjhi saazish' that sought to target the 'gaurav' of Gujarat. Modi also alleged that Lyngdoh was more interested in getting elections organized in Jammu & Kashmir than in Gujarat. In his public utterances, Modi would refer to Lyngdoh by his full name James Michael Lyngdoh, so that the people could immediately identify him as a Christian. Though the elections were being delayed, Modi was in a hurry to cash in on the sentiments that had come to the fore in the last few months. Therefore, with the support of the BJP at national level, he launched a multi-phase Gujarat Gaurav Yatra that would continue to roll right up to the elections. The yatra began on 6 September from a place in central Gujarat and, in phases, went to tribal areas of north and central Gujarat and other places: mostly those affected by the riots. Modi said that the yatra was meant to launch an agenda different from Godhra and post-Godhra. But his utterances left no one in doubt about what his game plan was. Reportedly, he started the yatra saying that the 'Congress cannot return to power wearing Italian spectacles' and charged that Sonia Gandhi was taking the advice of 'Rome's Pope'. Modi also berated Sonia for having said that Gujarat was becoming 'Godse's Gujarat'.

'The Congress, pseudo secularists and Musharraf are all speaking the same language,' he railed. 'None of them utter a word on Godhra but abuse Gujarat only for what happened afterwards.'

During the yatra, Modi made other controversial statements too. One such was 'paanch ke pacchis', an allusion to the high population growth amongst Muslims.

It soon seemed as though the BJP's top leaders themselves were becoming hostage to Modi's politics. Advani, who was elevated from home minister to deputy prime minister, declared that Modi was the best chief minister that Gujarat had ever had.

The election that followed was the most polarized that Gujarat has ever seen. Modi romped home with 127 seats in an assembly of 182, with a vote percentage of 49.85 of all votes polled. The Congress got only 51 seats but secured 39.55 per cent of all the popular votes.

A triumphant Modi took the oath at a grand ceremony at the Sardar Patel stadium in Ahmedabad in the presence of a huge turnout and VIPs, including Prime Minister Vajpayee. It now seemed as though the Gujarat chief minister was the supervisor of even the prime minister of India.

But given the huge number of organizations, groups, and individuals arraigned against him, Modi's troubles were far from over. They were not ready to absolve the strong man of Gujarat of any wrongdoing, just because he had emerged victorious at the elections. Organizations like Centre for Justice and Peace, headed by activist Teesta Setalvad, a Hindu Gujarati woman, were established to fight for justice for the riot victims.

The chinks in the armor of the blatantly biased Gujarat government's official machinery, in fact, opened the doors for those fighting for justice in the state.

When all the accused in the well-publicized Best Bakery Case were let off in July 2003 because the prosecution put up a poor case and the witnesses (under duress) turned hostile, eyebrows began to be raised in legal circles outside Gujarat.

Though the Best Bakery case was the 37th riot case in which the accused had been acquitted, none of the others were big enough to capture public imagination.

Referring to the 'administrators of Gujarat' (in a veiled reference to Modi and his men), the Supreme Court compared them to 'modern-day Nero', who were looking elsewhere when innocent children and helpless women were being assaulted, and probably deliberating on how the perpetrators could best be protected. The SC quashed the trial in the Best Bakery Case and directed a fresh re-trial in Maharashtra.

In March 2008, after long legal procedures, the Supreme Court set up a Special Investigations Team (SIT), headed by former CBI director R.K. Raghavan. In May 2009, the apex court ordered trials under the supervision of SIT in six major riot cases. The Supreme Court's order was in the interests of the criminal justice system and to address lacunae in the investigations and trials of these cases. The Godhra, Naroda Patiya and Gulberg Society cases were among the cases included in this batch. As noted before, the Godhra case came to fruition and so did the Naroda Patiya case. In August 2012 a total of 32 accused were convicted, including Modi's former minister, Maya Kodnani and Babu Bajrangi. In April 2012, a total of 23 persons were convicted in the Ode case and in July 2012, another 22 persons were convicted in the Dipda Darwaza case.

In September 2011 for the Gulberg Society case, Modi himself was called in for interrogation by the SIT. There were allegations that the slain MP, Ehsan Jafri, had even called up Modi for help. Modi denied both knowing Jafri and receiving a call from him. He also said that he had not referred to a 'Hindu reaction' at official meetings. As for the shifting of bodies from Godhra to Ahmedabad, Modi effectively put the blame on the district collector of Godhra, Jayanti Ravi, saying that she was not keen to keep the bodies in Godhra.

When confronted with his action-reaction statement (Godhra leading to post-Godhra), he said that it was a general statement, pointing that Gujarat had a long history of communal disturbances going back to 1714. He also made light of his *paanch ke pacchhis* statement, saying that it referred to the general problems of family planning and not to a specific community. At the end of investigations, the SIT let Modi off.

But the amicus curae in the case, Raju Ramachandran, stirred up a hornet's nest by stating that there was indeed some evidence under which Modi could be hauled up.

It can be safely predicted that the last of this matter has not been heard. The ghosts of Gujarat 2002 are likely to haunt Narendra Modi till his last days.

6

Vibrant Gujarat

Located in two different parts of New Delhi are the head offices of two organizations that have made it their business to promote trade and industry in India, and also India's exports to foreign countries.

The office of the Federation of Indian Chambers of Commerce and Industry (FICCI) on Tansen Marg, close to Bengali Market, is quite a landmark.

But the office of the Confederation of Indian Industry (CII) on Lodhi Road too, though tucked away in a side lane, is an important destination of many policy-planners and businessmen from India and abroad.

In his days as secretary of the BJP, Narendra Modi had scarcely paid attention to these organizations. It may have even escaped his notice that the two were locked in intense competition with each other to secure the 'goodwill' and patronage of the government. Strange as it may seem that this should be the case in post-liberalization India, FICCI and CII resorted to all sort of techniques to be closer to the government than the other. This was possibly a throwback to feudal India, when the 'mai-baap sarkar' prevailed.

By the turn of the century, it was the CII whose voice counted more with the central government than that of FICCI. Therefore, it may have come as a rude shock to the NDA government led by Atal Behari Vajpayee, that the CII stridently questioned the actions of the Modi government in 2002.

In fact, Gujarat cast a long shadow on CII's annual session in 2002 in New Delhi where the themes chosen included: 'Numbed Sensitivities: How Do We Dream Again?' And 'Social and Ethical Breakdown in India: What Should We As A People Do.'

Says a senior official of CII: 'These were thinly-veiled attempts to bring focus on the Gujarat affairs. Gujarat had shocked the conscience of the nation. Although we normally do not comment on political matters, many of our members were deeply agitated.'

The then leader of the Opposition, Sonia Gandhi, was also invited to the plenary session of the CII. Gandhi was forthright while commenting on the state of the nation: 'It is a colossal tragedy that globalization is accompanied by communal polarization,' she said.

Outside the meeting hall, the media was asking the then CII president, Sanjiv Goenka, whether the Gujarat riots would affect the flow of investments into India. Goenka was hard-pressed to answer that it would not be so, although he was not sure about what would happen to 'Destination Gujarat'.

However miffed the BJP bosses – even those critical of Modi – may have been at what the CII was saying, there was precious little that they could do.

But while CII was vociferous about Gujarat affairs, its rival FICCI kept quiet. This was a strategic silence, because FICCI realized that this was their big chance to get even with CII. After all, the government was that of NDA, of which BJP was the largest component, and they were not very happy.

FICCI's silence did not escape the attention of Narendra Modi; when he came back to power after the December 2002 elections, he realized that this rivalry between the two apex chambers could be exploited to his advantage.

'Modi figured out that he had won the elections but continued support of the people depended on a flourishing environment for business,' says a senior IAS officer from Gujarat. 'The people in Gujarat are very business-minded. As long as *dhando* (business) goes on unhindered, people are happy. If not, then they become restive.'

Although FICCI and its affiliate in Gujarat, the Gujarat Chamber of Commerce and Industry (GCCI) were silent, CII did not relent even after Modi won the state elections. CII tried to engage Modi at a national council meeting in Mumbai in late January 2003, but the meeting ended in a fiasco when an Oxford-educated historian, Jairus Banaji, entered the meeting. In the presence of Modi, Banaji thundered at the CII bosses: 'You can't have a strong economy without justice and the rule of law. Why is CII lending credibility to political forces that have blood on their hands?'

Banaji was whisked out of the hall, but Modi was not amused. His discomfiture grew when, a few weeks later, at a CII meeting in New Delhi on 6 February where he was present, senior CII member Rahul Bajaj talked about 2002 as being a lost year for Gujarat and asked Modi some tough questions.

Realizing that this CII offensive against Modi would not leave them and the state unaffected, leading businessmen of Gujarat who were on the same page as Modi, quickly grouped under a platform called the Resurgent Group of Gujarat (RGG) and convened a close-door meeting with office bearers of CII Gujarat, in what looked like a planned offensive.

RGG, that included top industrialists like Karsanbhai Patel of the Nirma group, Gautam Adani of the Adani group, Indravadan Modi of Cadila Pharma, and Chintan Patel of Ashima group, passed a resolution stating that 'some forces in national industrial federations have expressed untimely apprehensions without context about the law and order situation in the state.'

It also read: 'Forces causing embarrassment to the state globally need not misunderstand peace-loving and the tolerant nature of Gujarat as its weakness… All citizens of Gujarat involved in trade and industry have no other option but to rise to the occasion from a nonpolitical platform and condemn such efforts that damage the image of the state in the international arena.'

CII's local committee, who were, for all practical purposes on the same side of the fence as the members of RGG, considered passing a resolution against their national executive. Though this did not happen, some members indicated that they would like to resign from the CII. This set alarm bells ringing in the organization, perturbed as it was by the Government of India choosing FICCI as its partner in the newly-conceived Pravasi Bharatiya Divas started in January 2003. The Pravasi Bharatiya Divas was an initiative of the Government of India to woo non-resident Indians and people of Indian origin and make them part of the development of India. The CII was dead sure that they would be chosen to partner with the government for this programme. But the hawks within the government had prevailed in their view that the former should be taught a lesson and official patronage be bestowed on FICCI.

On 6 March 2003, CII's high-profile director general Tarun Das flew into Gandhinagar, met Narendra Modi and apologized to him. Tarun Das said: 'We are very sorry for the hurt that the chief minister has felt and we express regret for it.' He added: 'We have a strong commitment to Gujarat and we wish to renew the partnership between the government and CII to work together for the rapid growth, development and prosperity of Gujarat.' I called Das and asked him the need for an apology. Das, who was a bit defensive, said 'We can't offend a chief minister. My wife too asked me why I needed to apologize.'

With CII now neutered, Modi began engaging with FICCI to formulate a plan to aggressively market Gujarat, – especially to foreign investors. This was really not a new idea because ever since the advent of liberalization ten years ago, state governments had begun to woo businesses to their respective states. Under the license quota regime, the central government had always decided the location of investments and awarded licenses. But with the scrapping of licensing, state governments could now pitch for investments themselves. In fact so intense had the competition between the states become that it often resembled war. Modi decided that he would come out tops in this war in which Andhra Pradesh's Chandrababu Naidu was leading at the time. Modi realized that Gujarat had a natural advantage because the thriving non-resident Gujaratis (NRGs) business community could be roped in to boost the state's battered image abroad and to secure investments.

Out of this deep thinking emerged the idea of a 'Vibrant Gujarat' investment fair. In a sense, Modi was taking a leaf out of Chandrababu Naidu's book: Naidu had converted the sleepy, Nizami Hyderabad into a technology city with biggies like Microsoft setting up shop there and US President Bill Clinton even gracing the city during his short visit to India. All this was made possible by concerted and planned efforts at image building and hyping the reality. Incidentally, Naidu had been assisted in his efforts with generous dollops of assistance by the CII, who spread his message across the country and abroad and also provided him consultancy services.

Modi's tendency had always been to schedule programmes of the government when he believed, as he said, that 'the people's natural energy is high, usually around festival time.'

Vibrant Gujarat was timed to coincide with Navaratri, which is a major festival in the state. Diwali is an even bigger festival and coincides with the Gujarati New Year. But since people usually go on holiday at that time, Navratri was chosen instead. The show was to be organized in collaboration with the FICCI from 28-30 September 2003.

The grand inaugural ceremony was held on the banks of the Kankaria Lake in Ahmedabad. It was a cultural extravaganza attended by a host of Gujarati NRI businessmen.

When asked why he was combining the festival with hardcore business, Modi responded: 'During the daytime, we will deliberate on the future of Gujarat. At night, we will do *Shakti puja* [a reference to the invocation of Goddess Durga].'

Vibrant Gujarat marked a departure from the earlier investment policy followed by the state which had insisted on competitive bidding for various projects. Any project, even if granted to a business group, could be thrown open to 'challengers'. If the challenger offered better terms, the project could be handed over to him.

Under the new dispensation, there was a slew of projects on offer. Investors could sign an MoU (Memorandum of Understanding) with the government and go for them without any challenge.

'There were 135 projects on offer and we went for this route because competitive bids were seen as a big hurdle in attracting investments to the infrastructure sector which required huge sums,' says an official of the Gujarat government connected with Vibrant Gujarat.

At the business meetings, Modi flashed dollar dreams.'If you sow a rupee here, you will reap a dollar,' Modi said.

'People ask me why they should invest in Gujarat. I give them a simple answer. Gujarat is a policy-driven state with a peaceful labour culture. When the Planning Commission has fixed an annual target of 8 per cent for the country, for Gujarat the growth rate has been fixed at 10 per cent.'

Modi also predicted that in a few years, Gujarat would become the petrochemical capital of India. To make the Vibrant Gujarat show a success, Modi's government had announced a new industrial policy just a week ahead of the show.

Promises of investments poured in. There was, of course, some sleight of hand. Some investments already announced earlier were clubbed with new investment proposals. This made the total of investment proposals look more impressive.

In fact, promises of investment totalled ₹66,000 crore and 80 MoUs were signed. But 80 per cent of the investment proposals were from local companies which already did business in Gujarat: this included the Ambanis, who promised to put in ₹9000 crore in the next three years, ONGC, which promised ₹4000 crore to set up a petrochemical complex and Nirma (whose boss Karsan bhai Patel was part of the RGG industrialists) which declared its intent to put in ₹500 crore. An investment of ₹551 crore was also promised for a luxury cruise project. Promises included nine power proposals, nine in the chemical and petrochemical sector, and eight for special economic zones. FICCI's secretary general Amit Mitra was ecstatic. 'The amount of investment promised is huge,' he exclaimed. 'Even if it was for the entire country, I would have said this investment commitment is great. That it is for only one state makes it a stupendous achievement,' Mitra said.

But the Congress party's Shankarsinh Vaghela was skeptical. He declared that out of the ₹66,000 crore of investment declared, ₹26,000 crore of investment pledges had been made much earlier.

In one way, Vibrant Gujarat was a disappointment for Modi too.

He had wanted IT companies to pledge investments in the state. However, even though advance delegations had been sent to places like Bengaluru, this was not to be. Eventually, 33 of the 80 MoUs signed at the show were dropped: this came out at a review conducted by the Government of Gujarat eight years later in 2011.

But there was an important lesson learnt from the show: Modi had expected non-resident Gujaratis to flock to the show in large numbers. Although some had come, most others sent word that winter suited them better, because that coincided with the Christmas-New Year vacation season in Europe and the US.

So Modi, who was on the one hand buoyed by the success of the show, decided to continue with it by shifting the date. Therefore, to time it with the Uttarayan festival which coincided with Lohri in the north and Sankranti in the south, the 2005 edition of Vibrant Gujarat was held in early January.

The 2005 show was a more organized affair. Modi dispatched five ministerial delegations across the globe to solicit participation and investment. The areas of focus were information technology, agriculture, energy, gas, and petroleum. Many top industrialists like Mukesh Ambani, Shashi Ruia, Gautam Adani and the chairman of British Gas, Nigel Shaw, showed interest. The number of commitments to invest that were made at this show was much higher than at the 2003 Vibrant Gujarat. Investments of ₹106,160 crore were inked on paper through 227 MoUs. Out of this, there were 35 proposals for the port sector with investments of ₹15585 crore, 32 proposals for engineering and automobiles worth ₹16451 crore, and 24 proposals relating to the oil and gas sector for ₹13137 crore. According to the Gujarat government review of 2011, a total of 89 of the 227 MoUs were subsequently dropped, but 60 per cent of the MoUs signed during the first two editions of Vibrant Gujarat were realized. However, many analysts think that even a figure of 60 per cent is a gross overestimate.

'That the number of promises to invest were inflated is something that everybody knew, even those who were keen followers of Modi. But the show was a huge success in the sense that it brought back focus on Gujarat as an investment destination and not as a place where communal conflagrations happened,' says a prominent BJP leader from Gujarat.

The next edition of Vibrant Gujarat in 2007 – before the state elections scheduled later that year – was conducted on an even bigger scale. This time, delegations of prominent industrialists from the state were sent abroad. The message to potential investors was: 'In Gujarat there is no red tape, only a red carpet!' In an effort to underline the fact that Gujarat was the land of Gandhi, the show was kicked off with a multi-media exhibition 'Eternal Gandhi: The life and philosophy of the Mahatma.' Another exhibition titled 'Gujarat Discovered', showcased the strengths of Gujarat. Detailed investment opportunities in twelve focus areas were also prepared and offered to potential investors. These included power, oil and gas, chemical, petrochemical and pharmaceuticals, Special Economic Zone-led port and urban development, biotechnology, textiles and apparels.

At ₹461,835 crore and not unexpectedly, the quantum of investments promised in this edition of Vibrant Gujarat was four times as high as at the 2005 show. A total of 343 MoUs were signed, out of which 28 MoUs were investments aimed at special export zones (SEZs). The latter accounted for a total investment promise of ₹170889 crore.

The Vibrant Gujarat shows may have helped to promote the state as a wonderful investment destination but at the international level, it did little to remove the blot of the 2002 riots upon Modi. The point had been driven home clearly in March 2005 after the second Vibrant Gujarat show when Modi's visa to the US was cancelled by the Bush administration. Modi had held a ten year tourist/business visa for the United States since 1998, but when the Florida-based Asian American Hotel Owners Association (AAHOA), largely dominated by Gujarati motel owners in the US, invited him to address their annual convention, the Gujarat chief minister thought it fit to apply for a diplomatic visa. Though AAHOA had invited Modi, he knew that there could be trouble from a Coalition against Genocide (CAG) formed against him in the US. The moment news of Modi's invitation became public, CAG stepped up its campaign and lobbied in Capitol Hill. It appealed to Secretary of State Condoleeza Rice, to deny Modi a visa, accusing him of violating 'religious freedom' and building a cult like that of Hitler in Gujarat.

Nobody, including the CAG, seriously believed that the Bush administration – which was the only Western country to have not condemned the 2002 riots – would deny Modi a visa. As it turned out, not only did the Bush administration deny Modi a diplomatic visa but also cancelled his existing tourist/business visa. The latter was annulled invoking a section of the US Immigration and Nationality Act that allows the US government to deny a visa to any foreign government official who is responsible for 'a directly carried out at anytime, particularly severe violation of religious freedom.' The diplomatic visa was denied because it was held that the purpose for which Modi was coming to the US was 'not for a purpose that would qualify for a diplomatic visa.'

Even though they had lobbied for this, the denial of a visa exceeded the expectation of CAG. Modi and the BJP fumed and the UPA government in power made a feeble protest against the denial of the visa.'In 2005, there was severe stigma attached to Modi's name. The Bush administration was not ready to sully its image by allowing a person who had been accused of violating religious freedom and indicted by the National Human Rights Commission (NHRC) of India, into the US', says Errol D'Souza, professor at the Indian Institute of Management, Ahmedabad.

But Modi was not one to give up. Even while AAHOA was planning to cancel the invitation, pro-Modi elements in the organization set up web-casting facilities for Modi. Through this, Modi addressed the gathering from Gandhinagar on the appointed day. Besides inviting the Florida governor Jeb Bush (brother of US president George Bush) to Gandhinagar to experience Gujarati hospitality, Modi said: 'I am able to speak to you not just because of technology but because of the determination of your association to uphold democratic values and ignore motivated propaganda.'

Buoyed by his re-election in 2007, Modi attempted to take Vibrant Gujarat 2009 to an even bigger level. More so since the show came just months ahead of the 2009 general elections, during which, though not candidate for prime minister, Modi wanted to be recognized as a potential candidate in future. For the first time, Vibrant Gujarat had a foreign partner: Japan's External Trade Relations Organization (Jetro). The posters of Vibrant Gujarat saw Modi against the backdrop of flags of India and many other foreign economic powers and carrying the tagline: 'Global Dreams: One Destination.' About 600 foreign delegates from 45 countries came to the show where Modi announced triumphantly: 'Vibrant Gujarat had redefined economic crisis. You can see investment coming to Gujarat even in the backdrop of slowdown. Call it the vibrancy or stability provided by Gujarat.'

Acutely aware that he was facing criticism for inflating investment figures hugely and that much of the investment was not getting translated on the ground, Modi said: 'If an entrepreneur wants to invest here, we help him. There is not a single case where the investor has said we are withdrawing our project because we have problems with the government. If projects are not implemented, we are not responsible.'

During the event, 8662 MoUs promising investment totaling the huge amount of ₹1200000 crore (₹12000 billion) were signed. Industrialists gushed about Modi. Anil Ambani said: 'Gujarat is different from the rest of the country. The mood is different here.' But even the most unapologetic supporters of Modi realized that Vibrant Gujarat was nothing but a show to present a larger-than-life picture of the state and Modi himself. 'Industrialists say wonderful things about Modi, with their eye on various concessions for their investments like tax breaks and cheap land and water. The rush to sign MoUs is for the same purpose. At a later stage, many of these MoUs are not implemented because the excessive incentives that these businessmen want are not forthcoming from us,' a minister in the Modi cabinet said. 'These industrialists are also aware how Modi needs them for repositioning himself. They seek to take advantage of this.'

Though four editions of Vibrant Gujarat went a long way in lifting Modi's image as a champion of investment, he got a mega-boost due to two women: Mamata Banerjee and Nira Radia. The former was, at the time, the challenger in West Bengal seeking to dislodge the long-entrenched Left government. The latter was a public relations expert who was beginning to be recognized in the corridors of power in Delhi as a mover and shaker with contacts at high levels.

It had been Tata group chairman Ratan Tata's dream to produce a people's car at the cost of below ₹1 lakh for a long time. He embarked on the project to design the car in 2005: there would be no frills and the car would use less steel. Even as this was happening, Tata was wooed by the Left front government of West Bengal, which was keen to industrialize the state by inviting the new Tata car unit. Why

Ratan Tata was taken in by the Left *apparatchiks* is not known, but six sites were shown to his managers and the location finalized at Singur in Hooghly district. A final go-ahead was given to the Tatas on 18 May 2006. Trouble began in Singur soon thereafter: the land – 997 acres of farmland – was acquired by the government using an antiquated law. In the process, a huge number of farmers were displaced in the region where land is scarce and population pressure high. The land taken over was extremely fertile and allowed multiple cropping in a year. Mamata Banerjee of Trinamool Congress (TMC), looking to oust the Left front that had been in power since 1978, smelt an opportunity. She immediately started galvanizing opposition to the plant. Because the ousted farmers were already agitated, she did not have to try too hard. Soon, a cycle of protest and violence began. Ratan Tata realized that he had got caught in the crossfire between two political formations. He was not responsible for the mess because the land was not acquired by him. But he could do nothing, because he was very keen on producing the car. The situation escalated to a point of no return on 24 August 2008 when TMC began indefinite protests at the gates of the Nano factory and stopped all access to vehicles. Absolutely fed up, a few days later on 3 September, Ratan Tata declared that work – which had begun in 2007 – was being halted at Singur and that an alternative site would be scouted outside the state. 'I can't bring our managers and their families to West Bengal if there are going to be beaten, if there is going to be violence continually and if their children are afraid to go to school,' Ratan Tata announced.

Narendra Modi had been tracking the fate of Nano in West Bengal for long and he realized that if Ratan Tata could now be wooed to Gujarat, it would be a virtual coup. Since the riots, Ratan Tata did not hold Narendra Modi in great regard. He had to be cajoled by his public relations advisor, Nira Radia, to attend Vibrant Gujarat in 2005. Radia had great influence on Tata. In fact, he was so impressed with her public relations skills that he dismantled the public relations departments of all Tata group companies and handed over all accounts to Vaishnavi, Radia's PR firm. In the meantime, Radia had also been in touch with Modi for contracts for her PR outfit. While that did not materialize, the two became acquainted with each other, with the fact that Nira's husband was a Gujarati, helping her connect with Modi.

Even before Ratan Tata had announced a final decision to walk out of Singur, Modi men were in informal talks with Tata executives: the match-making role being played by Radia. As a result, Modi knew exactly how much and what sort of land Ratan Tata would seek for the Nano plant, and where its ideal location should be. On Modi's instructions, the Gujarat government did its homework at a frenetic pace and five sites in different parts of the state were prepared. This included one in Kutch, one each in south Gujarat and north Gujarat, and two close to Vadodara and Ahmedabad city respectively. By 2 October, a day before Ratan Tata formally announced that he was walking out of Singur, the site close to Ahmedabad had been finalized.

The *Times of India's* Ahmedabad edition ran a front page story on 3 October: 'Will Nano drive into Ahmedabad?' Swati Bharadwaj, the correspondent who filed the story, told me: 'On 2 October we got a tip off that the Tatas were coming with their Nano plant to Sanand, close to Ahmedabad. I went to Sanand and found that a huge tract of land of the Gujarat Agricultural University's cattle farm research station had been readied. Some earlier construction on the premises had also been halted. By talking to Gujarat government officials, we figured that this was, indeed, the site where the Nano plant would be relocated. But we played it safe by punctuating the headline with a question mark.' Two days later, the newspaper was so sure about the inevitable, that it carried an affirmative headline: 'Nano Will Be Made in Ahmedabad'.

After 3 October, there was a rush among state governments to offer sites to the Tatas. Teams came from Tata to various states like Maharashtra, Karnataka, and Andhra Pradesh. 'But we realized that their mind had been made up. They came to Hyderabad after giving us barely 12 hours notice and wanted to see land of a particular dimension, free of encumbrances and in the vicinity of the airport. The team had a cursory look at the land and went away. We could make out that the trip was a mere formality,' says a senior official of the industry department of the Andhra Pradesh government.

On 7 October, Ratan Tata formally announced that the car plant would come up at Sanand. 'An orphan without a home finds a home,' he announced. When asked about his journey from Bengal to Gujarat, he said: 'There is a bad M and a good M' (alluding to Mamata and Modi). A triumphant Narendra Modi – obviously exaggerating to make a point – said that it had cost him merely a one-rupee-SMS to Ratan Tata saying 'Suswagatam' – to get him to Gujarat, the moment the company had announced its withdrawal from West Bengal. Tata Motors managing director Ravi Kant was more realistic. When asked about the shift to Gujarat, he said that in merely ten days, the Modi government had readied land for possession, granted all approvals and permissions and offered a final deal. What Kant did not specifically mention is that the deal included a financial package that had really made it worthwhile for the Nano project to be relocated to Gujarat. This included sale of 1100 acres of land at a subsidized rate of ₹400 crore to be paid in installments over ten years, exemption on payment of stamp duty of ₹20 crore levied on the sale of land, deferred payment of Value Added Tax (VAT) on the sale for twenty years and a soft loan of ₹9750 crore at an interest rate of merely 0.1 per cent for setting up the project. The Gujarat government also took it upon itself to develop the infrastructure to the site including roads. It also sought to defray the cost of moving the machinery that the Tatas had already installed in their Singur factory to Sanand. Though the Modi government took special care to keep under wraps the details of the incentives offered, the opposition Congress claimed that the value of incentives totalled ₹30,000 crore.

Ratan Tata was so bowled over by the welcome he got that he said: 'When I came here first on an industry visit at the invitation of the Gujarat chief minister, I was told that I would be stupid if I did not have the Nano plant in Gujarat. But I am no longer stupid.'

Though the Opposition was baying at the deal, calling it a sell-out in which an entrepreneur was being given a huge incentive and being subsidized, Modi was happy. He knew this had been a masterstroke. Nano would be the greatest symbol of Vibrant Gujarat and this would go a long way in whitewashing his image that had taken a huge knock after the riots.

Modi has always been a deep thinking strategist: he envisaged that Nano could be used to develop the Ahmedabad area as a sort of Indian Detroit where more automobile industries could be attracted to set up their units. This would upstage Tamil Nadu which had hitherto the maximum number of automobile investments. 'The revolution brought by Henry Ford in the early twentieth century with its small car is now being replicated by Ratan Tata with his Nano,' Modi said. His words were prophetic.

Soon after being wooed by the Gujarat government, Ford Motors was knocking at the doors of Sanand for establishing a ₹4000 crore car and car engine manufacturing facility in July 2011. Land was allocated to them next to the Tata land at the rate of ₹1100 per square metre, payable in easy instalments. This was Ford's second plant in India, the first being in Tamil Nadu. What swung the deal were the incentives offered by the Gujarat government and the new location, which would allow the company to serve markets in other parts of India not close to Tamil Nadu. The realization that more than one car unit at a location would spur off development of ancillary units crucial to the industry that is dependent on outsourcing of various components, also made Ford plump for Sanand. Further, the port at Mudhra in Kutch too, from where cars could be exported, made Ford decide in favour of Gujarat.

After Ford, it was Peugeot's turn to look towards Sanand. As usual, Modi's government was welcoming with land and other incentives. But due to problems in Europe, the company put its plans on hold after taking possession of the land and laying a foundation stone.

However, Maruti Suzuki was attracted to Gujarat due to other reasons. Besides the incentives offered, the fact that Gujarat had a port got the top management of Maruti thinking. A unit in Gujarat would reduce the cost of transportation of the cars being exported from Maruti's unit in Haryana. A final decision on locating Maruti's new plant in Gujarat is yet to be taken. But Suzuki boss, Osama Suzuki, has met with Narendra Modi more than once.

Buoyed by the entry of Nano, Modi planned Vibrant Gujarat 2011 in an even bigger fashion. He was no longer interested in marketing Gujarat as a mere investment destination: Modi now wanted to position the state as a 'business hub where business and knowledge partnerships were forged especially in the areas of technology and innovation and also academics and the social sector.' One of Modi's ministers told me: 'We wanted to position Gujarat as the capital of business in India and to do this we cleverly used an allusion to Mahatma Gandhi who was Gujarat's son but had become the country's tallest spiritual and political leader.' Therefore, a new convention centre was constructed in Gandhinagar and named Mahatma Mandir. It was here that Vibrant Gujarat 2011 was organized. The results, in terms of agreements signed, were huge: 7936 MoUs envisaging investments of ₹2083000 crore were signed. An estimated 1400 foreign delegates were in attendance. The entire 'Who's who' of Indian business was there, singing paeans to Modi. 'The entire world looks to India and India looks to Gujarat,' declared Chanda Kochhar, managing director of ICICI, while Anand Mahindra, boss of the Mahindra group said: 'You cannot afford not to be here.' To Modi, Mahindra said: 'Tell your critics that you are doing a good job.'

While projecting Gujarat as the place to be in and the state that was the capital of investment and innovation, Modi seemed to be eking out a strategy that went beyond the mere offer of incentives.

In a sense, Vibrant Gujarat 2011 heralded the end of the international isolation of Modi. Although the US is yet to lift the visa ban on him, the growing business prospects in Gujarat made Her Majesty's Government make a scramble for Modi's doors. Though the UK had been boycotting Modi since 2005, when human rights groups had pressed for an arrest warrant against the Gujarat chief minister on the eve of a proposed visit to the country, in early October 2012, British foreign minister, Hugo Swire, directed the British High Commissioner to India, John Bevan, to call on Narendra Modi and end his boycott. A few British nationals – Muslims of Indian origin – had been killed in the 2002 riots, prompting UK human rights groups into action. After meeting Modi for nearly an hour, UK envoy Bevan said on 21 October 2012 that active engagement with Gujarat was necessary to advance British business interests in the state. Though he remarked that his meeting with Modi was not to be seen as an endorsement or a rehabilitation of the latter, the message was not lost on anybody. On his part, Modi restricted himself to a Tweet: 'Der aye durasta aye.' The turnabout in the British position was facilitated not only by the expanding business opportunities in Gujarat but also by a large number of non-resident Gujaratis in the UK, which had lobbied heavily for Modi.

Like he played off FICCI against CII, Modi now seems to be using the same strategy at the international level. With UK and US cool towards his government for long, Modi has, in the last few years, been assiduously wooing other countries like Japan and China outside the western liberal tradition as we will see in later chapter. During a visit to Japan in July 2012, Modi declared that he would set up a port city on the lines of Kobe. This would be located in Dholera, in the Gulf of Kutch, and not far from Ahmedabad. Modi announced that he envisaged $90 billion worth of investment in the Dholera Special Investment Region in the next ten years. This region would be spread across 903 square kilometres and include a Japanese industrial zone, a smart city, and other facilities. Modi also let it be known that he was planning to extend the proposed Delhi-Mumbai Industrial Corridor (DMIC) towards a coastal corridor from Ahmedabad to Dholera and Bhavnagar. (DMIC is a Japanese project connecting the political capital of the country to the financial capital with industrial hubs along the length.)

This grandiose plan is still on the drawing board, but Modi, whether his critics like it or not (and whether his promises have been delivered fully on the ground or not), has become the symbol of rapid economic progress.

7

Fear is the Key

In the end and as expected, Narendra Modi won. But he had romped home riding on the memory of Sohrabuddin Sheikh, who had been killed in a police encounter on 26 November 2005.

The final tally of the BJP in the Gujarat elections of 2007 was 117 seats in a house of 182. This was 10 seats less then what the Modi-led party had won in the 2002 elections. But there was no decline in the vote share of the party: BJP and Modi's support base in terms of percentage of total votes polled remained over 49 per cent. Everybody agreed that BJP won this huge majority and maintained its position after votes consolidated in Modi's favour. This happened after the 'Maut ke Saudagar' remarks made about him by Congress president, Sonia Gandhi. Launching a blistering attack against the Modi regime during an election campaign in Rajkot in the first week of December 2007, just a few days before polling day, Sonia said that those ruling Gujarat were 'liars and dishonest' and that they were 'maut ke saudagars (death traders)'. This was seen as a thinly-veiled reference to the killing of Sohrabuddin Sheikh and his wife that had become public knowledge barely six months ago. Sonia asserted that the Gujarat elections were not about one election but about 'protection of humanity, rule of law, and democracy.'

'It was a brilliant election speech and the lines were mesmerizing but what the Congress president did not realize was that the psyche of Gujarat was different from the rest of India. That what would have worked brilliantly outside Gujarat could backfire in this state,' says a senior Gujarat Congress leader who cannot be named. 'I am told that this epithet for Modi was coined by a leading Bollywood lyricist,' he adds.

Stung by the remarks, Modi immediately reacted in his election speeches: 'Do I need Sonia's permission to do anything?' he asked, upon which the crowds lustily cheered him and cried: 'No, no.' At another point there was a reference to Sohrabuddin Sheikh. When Modi asked: 'What should be done to people like him?' The crowds shouted: 'Kill him, kill him.' What followed in the next few days was a complete polarization of votes in favour of Modi. These remarks by Modi were referred to the Election Commission of India. But Modi wriggled out by saying that free and fair elections involved a debate on political issues in the marketplace of politics and that when statements are made by political opponents, others are entitled to respond to them.

Though Modi came out clean by sensing the public mood in Gujarat, the Congress was hard-pressed to justify (to the Gujarati voter) what Sonia had said. At first, senior leader Kapil Sibal was fielded by the party. 'The remarks made were not specific to Modi,' Sibal said. But barely a day later, Abhishek Manu Singhvi, Congress spokesperson, remarked that Sonia's comments were the 'most appropriate description of Modi.'

Sohrabuddin Sheikh, a notorious criminal belonging to Madhya Pradesh, was involved in various nefarious activities like inter-state smuggling and extortion. In November 2005, he was kidnapped by officers of the Gujarat police from a bus travelling from Hyderabad to Sangli and brought to Ahmedabad. Here, in a 'false encounter', he was killed in cold blood. His wife Kauserbi, who was with him on the bus, was also killed – reportedly in a farm house in Gandhinagar. The matter would have remained under wraps but for Sohrabuddin's brother, who, with a habeas corpus petition, moved the Supreme

Court. The apex body ordered an inquiry to locate the whereabouts of Sohrabuddin. It is then that the facts tumbled out: how the Gujarat police was keeping tabs on Sohrabuddin, how it rushed to Hyderabad upon learning he was there, and how it meticulously organized the kidnapping, with the help of elements of the Andhra Pradesh police acting in private capacity, possibly for a fee.

In the face of stiff opposition from the ruling establishment, the inquiry was first conducted by the Gujarat police's CID and handed over to the CBI.

In April 2007, two senior officers of the Gujarat police, deputy inspector general of police, D.G. Vanzara and superintendent of police, Rajkumar Pandian were arrested along with M.N. Dinesh, a superintendent of police from Rajasthan. Though Modi may have been unaware of the plot to get Sohrabuddin, Inspector General Vanzara was one of his favourites. Much to the chagrin of his superiors, the arrests were made by a bold Gujarat police officer, Rajnish Rai. In 2010, by which time the case had been handed over to the CBI, Gujarat's home minister Amit Shah was also arrested. It is said that Sheikh had probably been bumped off because he was extorting large sums from the marble lobby in Rajasthan, who then approached 'their friends' in Gujarat to 'help out'. Kauserbi, the wife of Sohrabuddin, was done away with, because she was witness to her husband's killing and keeping her alive would have been fraught with risk.

Sonia Gandhi's comments about the *maut ke saudagar* came in December 2007, barely seven months after the arrest of the police officers. She had averred that the public of Gujarat would be very upset to learn that senior police officers, whose duty it was to uphold the law, were participants in a case of kidnapping and the murder of Kauserbi, who was absolutely innocent of whatever her husband may have been guilty of. But Sonia did not know that, in the interim, Modi's men had raised the temperature in Gujarat by labeling Sohrabuddin Sheikh a Lashkar-e-Toiba (LeT) operative working at the behest of bosses in Pakistan and on a mission to eliminate a top leader from the state (Modi himself). This propaganda had resulted in many denizens of the state appreciating the killing of Sohrabuddin.'When Sonia made the comments, voters felt that Modi's government was being criticized by her for killing an enemy of the nation. They were distressed. With Modi and his men capitalizing on the opportunity, the BJP polled more votes than expected and romped home,' says the state Congressman.

'The fear of the enemy from across the border looms large among the people of Gujarat and this feeling of insecurity has intensified since the Godhra train incident,' says social activist Hanif Lakdawala. Various incidents occurring at regular intervals have served to strengthen this fear. On 15 June 2004, a nineteen-year-old Mumbai girl, Ishrat Jahan along with three men, Javed Ghulam Sheikh (alias Pranesh Pillai), Amjad Ali Rana, and Zeeshan Johar were encountered by the Ahmedabad police's crime branch on the outskirts of the city. The police story was that these four persons were actually operatives of the LeT who were on a mission to assassinate Narendra Modi. The police team was led by the same D.G. Vanzara, who had headed the operation against Sohrabuddin. The denizens of Gujarat bought into the police story – more so because the LeT purportedly owned up to the assassination plot. Many years later it was found that the four were killed in an encounter the night prior to 15 June and that they had no connection with the LeT and obviously no plan to kill Modi. It was disclosed that the four were possibly lured into Gujarat by the crime branch itself. In January 2003, barely two weeks after Modi returned to power after the riots, Sadiq Jamal Akhtar was killed in a police encounter. The police said that Akhtar, a LeT operative, had sneaked into Ahmedabad to assassinate Modi. But ten years later when Modi won Election 2012, six Gujarat police officials were arrested by the CBI, which declared that Akhtar's killing had been a staged encounter. The CBI also disclosed that Akhtar had been handed over to the Ahmedabad police who then killed him in cold blood.

There were some other incidents in which the LeT cropped up yet again, including a bomb blast at Kalupur railway station of Ahmedabad that led to ten people being seriously injured. Investigations concluded that it was the handiwork of LeT operatives seeking their revenge for the 2002 riots. The Akshardham incident in September 2002, right after the riots, played a big role in establishing this belief amongst people. On 24 September 2002, two armed intruders scaled the walls of the Akshardham temple – a modern shrine and cultural centre set up by the Swaminarayan Sanstha in Gujarat's capital Gandhinagar, not too far from Modi's residence. They began shooting at an assorted crowd of pilgrims and other visitors. The intruders were killed only after an overnight siege by the Black Cat commandos of the National Security Guard (NSG), who were flown in from Delhi. But this was not before thirty-three innocent visitors had been killed by the intruders. The gunmen were not properly identified but were said to be Pakistanis of the LeT, who had been sneaked into India through Kashmir.

'The Gujarat riots of 2002 actually went a long way in instilling a fear complex among the people. They began to apprehend revenge attacks from Muslims, especially after the siege of Akshardham,' says Vidyut Joshi, a sociologist.'But instead of blaming Modi for presiding over a regime that could do nothing to halt the riots, they started consolidating his position,' Joshi adds. The reasoning, according to the sociologist went like this: Muslim miscreants, perhaps encouraged by subversive elements across the borders, had deliberately burnt the bogies of Sabarmati Express at Godhra that was carrying *kar sevaks*. This led to a Hindu reaction against Muslims. Modi allowed the Hindus to vent their feelings. Now that agents of Pakistan would try and target Hindus in Gujarat, only a 'He-Man like Modi' could stand up to them. The rest, especially Congressmen, were sissies who were going out of the way to pander to the minority which practiced the same religion as denizens of Pakistan. Bomb blasts in other parts of the country also had their impact on Gujarat. For instance, the bomb attacks on the Delhi–Lahore Samjhauta Express near Panipat in February 2007 that killed 68 persons, was attributed to the LeT and heightened the apprehension called in Gujarat. It was only many years later that the hand of a Hindu organization, Abhinav Bharat was detected behind the attack.

'*Ekaj hi mard manas che*': there is only one 'He-Man' in Gujarat and this is Modi. 'This was the feeling in Gujarat at least in the run up to the 2007 elections,' says journalist Harit Mehta. 'They saw him as their sole protector, the only man who could protect them in times of a siege.'

That this feeling was widespread and prevalent in post-2002 Gujarat. Between 2002 and 2005, from tea vendors, to auto-rickshaw drivers to office peons to top managers, believed that Modi was their only saviour. Such a belief was held by both men and women and cut across caste lines.

On his part, Modi also never lost an opportunity to raise the temperature on matters relating to terrorism and Pakistan. While addressing an anti-terrorism rally organized by the BJP in Mumbai in 2006, he said: 'This UPA government is soft on terror and keeps appeasing the minorities. They have also removed POTA.' The prevention of terrorism act (POTA) was a controversial provision on the statute that allowed confessions made by an accused in police custody to be admitted in a court of law. Invoking POTA, the police resorted to severe torture to extract confessions from accused persons, later using these to convict many who were possibly innocent or not entirely guilty. Since it was believed that POTA had been liberally used to convict accused Muslims, the UPA government, under pressure from human rights groups, repealed the Act soon after coming to office. When doing so, Prime Minister Manmohan Singh said that POTA was no deterrent to terrorist acts and pointed out how Akshardham had happened, in spite of POTA being on the statute book at that time. In July 2006, Modi responded thus: 'The prime minister says that Akshardham happened in spite of POTA. I say that it is only due to POTA that the perpetrators have been hanged (sentenced).'

He made the remark soon after a special court had awarded capital punishment to two accused involved in the case (though POTA had been repealed, the draconian law was still admissible in old cases already committed to the court). Though the two gunmen who had opened fire on the pilgrims were killed in the encounter with NSG, the two convicted were their associates who were involved in the conspiracy.

'I am the chief minister of a border state and in the case of an attack from Pakistan, I will be the first to face Mian Musharraf,' Modi declared at the same anti-terrorism rally, raising the spectre that an attack by Pakistan army through the Kutch route was a possibility.

His speech electrified the public in Gujarat who have nursed an unvoiced fear about Pakistan, which was accentuated when the chief minister of the state, Balwant Rai Mehta, was killed when the aircraft in which he was travelling was brought down by fire from the Pakistani air force. Mehta, who was accompanied by his wife and other civilians including a journalist, was flying over Bhuj in September 1965, while the Indo-Pakistan war was on. Incidentally the founder of Pakistan, Mohammed Ali Jinnah himself, was a Gujarati Muslim. This also contributed towards creating disenchantment against Pakistan among Gujaratis.'Though Gujarat had not been partitioned like Bengal and Punjab and did not receive refugees barring Sindhis, the feeling against Pakistan was always stronger in the state than, in say, Bengal,' says A.D. Dave, a retired government official.

Modi also continually stressed how the Government of India had refused assent to the Gujarat Control of Organized Crime Act (GCOCA), in spite of the state assembly clearing it in April 2003. By the time the bill had gone for presidential assent, the UPA government was in power and the home ministry advised the president not to give clearance because of its controversial provisions. 'It was projected to the general public as though the provisions of the Act would be used against anti-socials and terrorist groups, many of whom were from across the border. And as though by not clearing the Act, the UPA government was encouraging terrorism and holding back the hand of Modi who wanted to strongly battle terrorism,' says Ramesh Parekh, a teacher.

Though Pakistan had been formed only in 1947, the fear of invaders across the border had been ingrained in the psychological make-up of many Gujaratis because of older history. Continual raids by Mahmud of Ghazni in the eleventh century on Gujarat and specifically on the ocean-front Somnath Temple, had become a part of Gujarati folklore. This identity was catalyzed by the works of a Congress leader Kanaiyalal Munshi, who was also a lawyer and a writer. He later became a minister in Bombay state and even later the governor of UP. When the Nizam of Hyderabad was deposed through Police Action in 1948, Munshi was the Agent-general of India in Hyderabad. He also started the Bharatiya Vidya Bhavan. It was Munshi, who, for the first time used the term 'Gujarati Asmita' at a literary conference in 1940. Munshi wrote a few historical novels like *Jaya Jaya Somnath*, *Gujarat No Nath*, *Rajadhiraj* and *Patan Ni Prabhuta*. Greatly influenced by the French writer Alexander Dumas, the novels of Munshi were set in medieval Gujarat when the region was ruled by Hindu rulers. This was before the Delhi sultans and the Mughals made incursions into Gujarat. Some modern historians claim that the novels of Munshi were based not on events as they happened, but on beliefs about what had happened centuries ago. Correct or not, the books had the result of glorifying the Hindu rulers of the Gujarat region. Munshi's books were very popular and lapped up eagerly by the middle classes. The contents of the book, came to define the beliefs of an average Gujarati reader about the glory of Gujarat that had been destroyed by invaders.

'Gujarat is a very inclusive society but for the fact that middle and upper classes don't take Muslims into consideration in this inclusiveness. This feeling has been there for long, but accentuated after the 1990s,' says S.J. Balasubramanian, an academician who migrated to Gujarat thirty-five years ago. He points out that in the normal scheme of things, Gujarati Hindus and Muslims have good business relations, but not 'personal relationships'. Hindu business owners have no qualms about employing Muslim workers or artisans and freely trading with Muslim merchants. 'But it is rare to find a Hindu having a Muslim friend, and vice versa. Inter-marriages are virtually unknown and hardly ever will a Hindu or a Muslim venture to the homes of each other. But they coexist wonderfully and also collaborate when required,' adds Balasubramanian. A good example of this cooperation was seen after the killer earthquake of 26 January 2001 which left over 13,000 dead. 'At that time, no animosity was seen between the two communities and each helped the other in the hour of crisis,' says Swati Sucharita, a journalist who lived in Gujarat at the time. Muslims comprise a little over 9 per cent of Gujarat's population. Interestingly and unlike many other parts of India where Muslims have Urdu as their mother tongue, the Gujarati Muslim speaks Gujarati. Except for the meat that they eat, Gujarati Muslim food is also the same as that of his Hindu counterpart. 'In that sense, the Gujarati Muslim is integrated into Gujarat's society. And yet, 'Gujarati Asmita' as defined, does not include the Gujarati Muslim. This is strange, to say the least,' points out Hanif Lakdawala. The Bohris, who have flourishing businesses across the nation originate from Gujarat and still live there in large numbers. 'It is a conundrum as to why the Muslims are not considered an integral part of Gujarati society,' laments Tanvir Koreishi, a senior corporate executive. Sociologists say that in addition to contents of historical novels becoming part of folk-lore, the fact that there was no Hindu–Muslim engagement through the ages other than in business, may have contributed to this state of affairs. 'When you know somebody closely, you learn to trust him. If you do not know him, fear preys on your mind and out of this fear arises insecurity. Precisely that has happened in Gujarat,' says a senior IAS officer who has been in the state for thirty years. 'There has been no Ganga–Jamuna confluence of cultures, like in north India. Gujarat was far from Delhi and the benefits of Mughal rule, like a stable government and stable administration that led to the flowering of culture in north India, was never felt in the region. There has also not been the rise of a caste like the Kayasths of north India (traditionally bureaucrats), who contributed a lot to the fostering of a secular culture and bringing the two communities closer.'

'Gujarat's long coastline has always bred a sense of entrepreneurship and commerce in its people. That is why there has been a Hindu–Muslim business engagement,' the officer continues.

The fact that the Gujaratis have always been a mercantile community also means that in relative terms, society does not afford equal value to jobs in the army or police.

'Everybody wants to be part of commerce and trade. Very few people want to join the military or the police,' points out former director-general of police, R.B. Sreekumar. 'Till the mid-1970s, even recruits to the state police service had to be sourced from northern states, because virtually no Gujarati was interested in joining the police force,' says R.N. Bhattacharya who also retired as a director-general of police. Had the Gujaratis been a strong martial race, it is possible that this feeling of insecurity would not have taken root easily, feel many observers.

Other than this insecurity and the resultant inability to include the Muslims as an integral part of society, Gujarat is an ideal place. Outsiders who have lived in Gujarat say that they have never felt out of place in the state. 'We have always felt welcome and have been coopted into society with open arms,' says Subroto Bhowmik, an artist and designer who has lived in Ahmedabad for forty-five years. 'People are warm, hospitable and ready to help. They never make you feel like an outsider,' adds Swati Sucharita.

Although this fear complex helped Modi retain his popularity in Gujarat till the 2007 elections, subsequent events clearly indicate that things changed thereafter. On 26 July 2008, 21 bomb blasts hit Ahmedabad in a period of 70 minutes. The blasts were of low intensity, and yet resulted in 57 deaths. Most of the bombs were planted in tiffin boxes on cycles, or on public transport. The blasts were intelligently planned to cause maximum damage: two happened in hospitals: the second just when those injured from the first blast were being brought inside for treatment.

About five minutes before the first blast, several news agencies received a 14-page e-mail titled 'Await five minutes of revenge of Gujarat 2002.' The blasts were exactly in the pattern of a similar explosion in Jaipur a month-and-a-half earlier, and a failed attempt in Bengaluru the previous day. The Indian Mujahadeen was held responsible for both the blasts.

Though there was anger at the explosions which Modi rightly termed a 'crime against humanity,' there was no reaction or a heightened fear perception. Says Amrit Dave, a retailer: 'People took it as a normal risk to life and nothing unique to Gujarat. People in many states like UP, Rajasthan, Maharashtra, or Karnataka were subject to the horrors of bomb blast and Gujarat was not singled out'.

Here's what an industrialist said: 'The people of Gujarat were getting fed up with the politics of hate and had become wary. They refused to get incited or cowered down by such incidents.' Indications that the blasts had not polarized sentiments in favour of Modi came a few months later in 2009, when general elections were held. The BJP won 15 out of the 26 seats in Gujarat, leaving the Congress to secure 11 Lok Sabha berths. If the mood had swung more decisively in favour of Modi, the BJP might have ended with probably 20 seats or more.

'The winds of change began blowing around 2009. As the benefits of higher economic growth in the period 2004-08 began to trickle down, people became concerned about other things. There was a discernible change in mindsets. People became more confident about their future and less taken in by propaganda about dangers from across the border,' says analyst Leena Misra. She also feels that people became more focused on bread-and-butter issues and less on temples and the like. 'People were becoming more tolerant and even the strong intolerance that the average Gujarati has towards non-vegetarianism, was getting diluted.'

On their part, Modi's managers also began to focus less on Hindutva issues and more on development, hailing Modi as a 'Vikas Purush', or, 'development man.' Even in the run up to the 2007 polls, Modi had been given that epithet. But his image of being a '*Hindu hriday samrat*' the 'king of Hindu hearts' – was stronger in public perception. 'Perhaps realizing the shift in public mood, Modi's managers also began to think that it would not be a bad idea for him to co-opt Muslims into his scheme of things,' says a senior secretary to the Government of Gujarat.

Little wonder then that two years later, Modi embarked on the mission of Sadbhavana, specifically to woo Muslims. But how and why Sadbhavana failed, is another story.

8

The Sadbhavana Experiment

Narendra Modi's prime ministerial ambitions had become clear to discerning observers in 2004, but by 2009 a large number of people were convinced that the Gujarat *nu nath* (literally the overlord of Gujarat) had his eyes set firmly on New Delhi. Therefore, the popular expectation was that some Muslim names would find their place in the list of BJP candidates for the 2012 assembly elections. After all Modi could be called an 'inclusive leader' – a prerequisite for being the chief in Delhi – only if there were at least some minorities in his camp. However, not a single Muslim candidate was fielded. This came as a surprise also because Modi had been assiduously wooing Muslims (or going through the motions of doing so) since the last general elections in 2009. 'In the end, Modi comprehended that fielding Muslims would make him vulnerable to attack by extreme Hindu organizations, which are any way cut up with him for not furthering the Hindu agenda. He did not want to take any chances in the tightly-contested election, given that Keshubhai's Gujarat Parivartan Party was also in the fray,' says a senior BJP leader. 'He reckoned that while the Muslims would not vote for him anyway, the Hindus would shy away from any Muslim candidates fielded by the BJP and that there was therefore little point in giving seats to them.'

In the heat of electioneering, Modi went one step further. Still not sure that he would get a massive mandate, Modi began singing his old tune and alluding to 'Ahmed Miyan'. This was a reference to Sonia Gandhi's political advisor, Ahmed Patel, who, he hinted, could become the chief minister of the state if the Congress came to power. Patel belongs to the Bharuch district of south Gujarat and in the '80s had represented the seat in Lok Sabha. With this rabble-rousing, Modi was back to square one, the point where he had begun.

At the end of February 2009, just before the general elections, Modi made his first symbolic move to woo Muslims. He appointed a Muslim as the director-general of police (DGP), the senior-most officer of the police department. By this, Sabir Khandwawala, a 1973 batch IPS officer became the first Muslim director-general of police in Gujarat. The appointment was effected by removing the incumbent police chief P.C. Pande, who was a hot favourite of Modi. Pande had been the police commissioner of Ahmedabad during the riots of 2002 and was, on the orders of the Election Commission, removed as DGP at the time of the 2007 elections. However, after Modi won the elections, Pande was restored to his position. In contrast, Khandwawala was in the doghouse before his elevation. His promotion had been delayed because he had been sentenced by a fast track court in 2003 to five years imprisonment in the case of custodial torture. Khandwawala was known to have been critical of the police administration and handling of the 2002 riots when he was in charge of training: a posting that is, in police parlance, regarded as a 'side-lined' posting. In 2007, finding his career in the police at a dead end, the officer had expressed a desire to quit service.

Once he was appointed, Khandwawala was to become a great favourite of Modi. So much so that after he attained the age of superannuation, Modi gave him a three month extension. At the end of this extension, Modi wanted to give him a second extension but failed. This was because the central government did not play ball. (Extensions to IAS and IPS officers have to be approved by the central government, since they are part of All India services). Though Khandwawala took up a private-sector assignment after retirement, the buzz is that he was an aspirant for a BJP assembly seat in the 2012 elections. However, this did not materialize. Another police officer, A.I. Saiyed, who retired as additional director general of police, was also an aspirant. Saiyed had, in 2010, been fielded by the BJP as a candidate for the position of mayor of Ahmedabad. Had he won, he would have become the first BJP Muslim mayor of the city.

The rehabilitation of Khandwawala and the opportunity provided to Saiyed are exceptions: Muslims in Gujarat do not, by and large, see themselves as favourites in Modi's regime.

'A significant section of Muslims have reconciled with their circumstances and now want to go ahead with their lives,' Hanif Lakdawala says. 'It does not mean that the memories of 2002 do not hurt. Even as the battle to bring to justice the perpetrators of 2002 continues, Muslims have realized that *agey badna hi zindagi ka naam hai*' (to move forward is life), he adds. A good example of this is Qutubuddin Ansari, a twenty-eight-year-old tailor, whose photograph with terror writ large on his face and folded hands imploring the police to save him from marauding mobs, became the defining image of Gujarat 2002. After moving to many different places like Malegaon and Kolkata, Ansari has come back to Ahmedabad to build a new life for himself. He continues to be a tailor and lives with his wife and three children. Things are decidedly better for him today. And yet, Ansari avoids the public glare and would rather not talk about Gujarat 2002.

'The Muslims of Gujarat have today become more self-reliant than before. They do not depend on the government. They want to be in charge of their own destiny and are opening their own schools and creating their own employment opportunities,' says Mohammed Hussain, a small businessman. 'Yes, they are happy that there is no active discrimination against them by the state government as there was in 2002. Also, the fact that the Central government is headed by a secular formation gives them a kind of reassurance that was not there in 2002. But to say that the Muslims of Gujarat have become fans of Modi is a palpably false statement to make.'

Many Muslims also feel that with the amount of international pressure that Modi had to face post-2002, he will ensure that no riots ever happen in Gujarat again.

'In fact, 2002 is the greatest insurance that something like that will not recur,' says Raheel Dhattiwala, an academic. A.I. Saiyed, retired additional director general of police, who has joined the BJP is quoted in newspaper interviews as saying that he would want Muslims to become part of the mainstream and not remain categorized as a homogeneous, uneducated class which refuses to assimilate into the larger society.

Coincidentally, the first sign that the Muslims wanted to make peace came around 2009. 'In the past, they were nurturing hopes that Modi would fall in elections or be removed. But when this did not happen, they began reconciling,' says Hanif Lakdawala.

In January 2010, the newly-appointed rector of Darul Uloom and a Muslim from south Gujarat, Maulana Ghulam Muhammad Vastanvi, set the cat among pigeons by suddenly stating that 'Muslims had economic opportunities in Modi's Gujarat.'

'Let's move on,' he said. 'The riots happened eight years ago and today, Muslims are beneficiaries of development in Gujarat.'

Pandemonium broke out immediately after Vastanvi's statement. So massive were the protests – the students of the seminary virtually revolted – that Vastanvi had to quit his job within days. He also issued a statement: 'I cannot forgive Narendra Modi. Allah will not forgive Narendra Modi.'

The jury is still out on why Vastanvi had initially decided to give Modi a clean chit.

While the protests made him retract the endorsement of the Modi raj, Muslim analysts aver that perhaps he was looking for land to set up a university in Gandhinagar. The fact that the Gujarat chief minister was open to land allotments to industry had perhaps prompted the statement. While the authenticity of this interpretation cannot be verified, the possibility that Vastanvi was being sincere, cannot be discounted either.

Though Vastanvi is not of the Bohra community, the first efforts at reconciliation were led by the Bohris Muslim businessmen, most of whom converted en masse to Islam from Hinduism many centuries ago. Hard-core Sunnis do not consider Bohris as Muslims, because some of their practices are akin to those of their Hindu ancestors. But as pragmatic businessmen, the Bohris (which means that they belong to the Bohra, or trading community), concluded that continual tension with the powers-that-be would be disastrous for the community and it therefore made sense to reconcile with them. Encouraged, Modi also went out of the way to woo the Syedna, the spiritual head of the Dawoodi Bohra community, and called on him in Surat on his birthday. The Syedna, it appears, was floored by the Modi gesture and for the 2012 election, made it known that Bohris should vote for him. Along with the Bohris, other Muslim business communities like the Khojas (who follow Aga Khan) also softened their stand against the Modi regime. 'This is hardly surprising because business requires patronage,' says Hasan Jowher, an activist and a banker based in Ahmedabad.

It was a year-and-a-half after Vastanvi made and withdrew the controversial statement and on Modi's birthday on 17 September 2011 the Gujarat CM initiated his Sadbhavana mission, billed as one to get all communities living in Gujarat together. The birthday was a welcome excuse to launch the mission. But Modi was actually capitalizing on what he thought was a window of opportunity opened by Supreme Court observations made less than a week earlier.

The apex court had said that it would not monitor the Gulberg Society case anymore and decided to leave it to the trial court to decide whether Narendra Modi needed to be investigated further in the matter.

As narrated in an earlier chapter, over 70 persons including former Congress MP Ehsan Jafri had been killed at Gulberg Society, one of the most gruesome incidents in the post-Godhra riots. Jafri's wife had petitioned the apex court in 2007, that Modi and others had colluded in preventing timely help to save the residents of Gulberg Society.

Upon hearing the SC's order, Modi immediately tweeted: 'God is great', while his allies announced that the Gujarat chief minister had finally been given a clean chit.

True to his trade mark style, Modi finalized the Sadbhavana as a high-profile show, with BJP dignitaries invited from all across the country. At the widely-televised event, Modi sat on a three-day fast, announcing that 'my government does not work for the majority or minority, it works for 6 crore Gujaratis.' Recalls Sudhir Shah who went to the fasting centre at the huge convention hall of the Gujarat University in Ahmedabad: 'It was a great public relations exercise and a grandly organized show with halls full of delegates and giant television screens set up for easy viewing'.

Even BJP leaders like Sushma Swaraj, not known to be great fans of Modi, were forced to make appropriate noises: 'Modiji has been ruling with *sadbhav* for the last ten years.' Although the Sadbhavana show generated a lot of bytes, Modi was, at one stage, caught on the wrong foot when a Muslim cleric from a small dargah on the outskirts of Ahmedabad, Syed Imam Shahi Saiyed, offered Modi a skull-cap and asked him to put it on his head. Modi refused the skull cap – a Muslim religious symbol – and instead asked for a shawl. The Imam came out of the convention hall and told waiting newspersons that Modi had been exposed and that the refusal to accept the cap was 'not an insult to me but an insult to Islam.' BJP spokespersons were hard-pressed to defend Modi and made noises that thousands of Muslims had come calling on the fasting chief minister and nobody had offered a skull cap to him, so why the insistence by this Imam? They also said that the fast was to focus on the matter of development and how it touched all. It was certainly not about appeasement of minorities, they said, repeating the standard line of the saffron party.

Modi was, however, unfazed by the turn of events. At the end of the show, he proclaimed that this was only the first of his Sadbhavana fasts and that he would hold 36 one-day fasts across the state to spread the message of Sadbhavana. Modi kept his word and concluded his Sadbhavana Yatra five months later – on 16 February 2012 – at the *shaktipeeth* of Ambaji, known for its Durga temple. Those who observed the show from close quarters said that the yatra was nothing but a political juggernaut on the move, for which all the resources of the state government had been roped in to project the personal image of the chief minister. However, Modi himself wrote in his blog that the experience of interacting with people and observing one-day fasts across all districts in Gujarat was extraordinary. His admirers too compared his fasts to *aswamedh yagnas* of yore, which kings performed to prove their supremacy. 'Modi's *aswamedh* was to conquer the hearts of people of all communities,' asserted one Modi supporter.

But his detractors were not convinced. Former chief minister Suresh Mehta, now with Keshubhai's Gujarat Parivartan Party, filed RTI applications and found out that the Gujarat government (and not the BJP) had paid ₹10.42 crore to the Gujarat State Road Transport Corporation as payment for hiring 7270 buses for the yatra.

'At most places, work in the district administration would come to a halt for a week before the fast and all resources were being used for the massive bandobast. This included leveling of the ground and making arrangements for buttermilk for those participating in the fast along with Modi,' said a journalist covering the Sadbhavana trail. 'The bandobast was mind-boggling, considering that the fasts were held in the presence of thousands of visitors brought in to express solidarity.'

The speeches that Modi made at the fasting centres were anything but conciliatory. They were basically designed to bash the Congress party. Mostly, Modi would dwell on how the Congress party sought to divide and rule the country in the fashion of the British whom they succeeded, and on how this divide-and-rule had caused irreparable damage to the image of 'our great nation.'

In the course of his inflammatory oratory, Modi would invariably move to the subject of governance in Gujarat and point out how his state had 'shunned vote-bank politics for the politics of development'. Modi would assert that due to collective efforts, inclusive growth had replaced the age-old, divisive practice of 'divide-and-rule' in Gujarat.

At other stages of his oratory, Modi would spew fire on how fifty years of Congress rule was anti-people, and how Congress leaders had got accustomed to throwing crumbs at the voters and making tall promises. At other places, he would assert that the Gujarat government also topped in implementing the Centre's 20-point programme for the last consecutive ten years. 'The Congress is building a vote-bank, we are building houses for people below the poverty line,' he said, at another Sadbhavana event. At a third, Modi spewed: 'They cannot see Muslims, Christians, and people of other religions working together in Gujarat. The handful of people who are against Gujarat are baffled by the success of Sadbhavana.'

But Imtiaz Ali (name changed), a corporate executive, is not convinced. 'If there is Sadbhavana in Gujarat, this is because of the Muslims, not Modi,' he asserts. Imtiaz, who had considered migrating elsewhere in India in the aftermath of the riots, ultimately decided to stay back in Ahmedabad. 'I agonized for months but this was my home, where I had grown up and studied. Why should I run away? Imtiaz confesses that before 2002, he went to mosques irregularly. But after the riots, he has sought solace in the Koran and has developed a Muslim identity.

Banker M.H. Jowher says that Muslims have made peace and the aggressors of 2002 have allowed them to do so, because of the realization that Muslims are an important cog in the economic machine that is Gujarat. 'Many trades like driving, auto part repair, and tailoring are dominated by Muslims who have expertise that runs over generations. Where would you get their replacement?' Jowher asks. In the immediate aftermath of the riots, there was an attempt made by the aggressors to dislocate the Muslims from these trades and bring in others. But the effort failed.

'As far as Muslims are concerned, if they are reconciled to be second-class citizens of Gujarat then it is not a problem for the aggressors of 2002. And that's what's happening,' says Jowher. 'If a journalist randomly asks Muslim taxi-drivers or small traders on the roads of Ahmedabad or Vadodara what they think of Modi, they will speak positively about him. But do not get taken in by this. They do not speak out their mind because they do not know who they are speaking with,' says Imtiaz.

Activist Shabnam Hashmi, who has been working for the rehabilitation of Muslim women in Gujarat, also believes that things have not really changed for the minorities. 'Yes, the Muslim business community has given up its opposition to Modi for practical reasons. For others, things remain much the same,' she says. Many Muslims feel that they have to become part of the greater society, if only to reduce their vulnerability. Of course, they say that it is a moot point whether the Muslims were the ones to refuse to get assimilated or whether they were forced into ghettoes by the majority community. An example of the state of affairs pertaining to minorities in the Modi Raj, is the story of a Hindu bungalow owner who proposed to sell his property to a Muslim in the city of Bhavnagar in Saurashtra in early 2012. As news spread about the impending deal, the bungalow owner found agitators outside his house every day, chanting 'Ram dhun'.

The ritual, which was reported in newspapers, continued till the bungalow owner rescinded his plans to sell the house to a Muslim. When I asked a Muslim businessman who lives in the Paldi locality of Ahmedabad what the 'feel good' factor in Gujarat meant for him, he said, 'Earlier, there were many slums near my home on the Sabarmati river bank. Those have been now removed and the area looks pleasant. You can say this is a "feel-good" factor for me,' he said.

In another telling instance, Narendra Modi refused to implement in Gujarat a Central scheme, whereby scholarships are given to bright but needy pre-Matric Muslim students. Through the scheme, 75 per cent of the scholarship money is provided by the Central government with 25 per cent funding by the state government. GOI had earmarked ₹9.82 crore for awarding 52,260 scholarships, the recommendation for which came from the Sachar Committee, appointed to assess the status of Muslims. The refusal of Modi to implement the scheme is now a subject matter of legal dispute in the Gujarat High Court. The Modi government's stand is that it is not in favour of giving goodies based on the criterion of religion and therefore will not implement the scheme.

Disbursement of the scholarships was, however, aimed at helping the Muslims in Gujarat be a part of the mainstream. According to Abusaleh Shariff, this would be necessary. The economist with the NCAER and secretary to the Sachar Committee had found that poverty amongst Muslims in Gujarat is eight times that among caste Hindus and 50 per cent more that OBC Hindus, SCs and STs. The Sachar Committee itself had found that 60 per cent of Gujarat's Muslims lived in urban areas and were mostly self-employed. This would mean that they were less-employable, making a case for more empowerment.

Since analysts believe that Modi will be running for the prime minister's post in the next general elections, what Muslims outside Gujarat think about his Sadbhavana is also relevant. A general survey in many cities of India like New Delhi, Hyderabad, and Mumbai reveals that Muslims here believe that justice has not been delivered to their brethren in Gujarat. But nonetheless, they are finding their feet again in Modi's state. 'It has nothing to do with Modi. It is because of the resilience of people – Hindu or Muslim – to survive the most adverse of circumstances. And the Muslims of Gujarat have not only survived but their prospects have begun to look up,' says Anwarul Huda, director general, law and order of Andhra Pradesh police in Hyderabad. He points out that in the aftermath of the Police Action of 1948 when India took over Hyderabad, thousands of Muslims were killed. But Muslims again found their feet. 'Basically most of the people of the other community are good. This is the case in Mumbai, Ahmedabad or wherever. This also acts as insurance for the Muslims of Gujarat,' Huda adds. 'Possibly Gujarat 2002 was an aberration, at least that's what I hope it is,' says a Muslim professor in New Delhi. He also points to how Hindus and Muslims had worked together in the rehabilitation work after the Gujarat earthquake of 2001.

Some others were circumspect and said that with politics becoming more competitive in India, hate and divisiveness will increasingly be taken recourse to by political parties. 'The Muslims are an easy target. They are always at the receiving end,' says Shakeel Ahmed, a doctor from Delhi. Social activists like Asghar Ali Engineer have continually harped on the twisted history lessons imparted in text books as the source of the problem. His conclusion: so long as these books are not corrected and the distortions smoothened, the Modis of the world will continue to reign.

Most others, however, felt that with the rapid growth in Gujarat, the state's Muslims too have become beneficiaries of this process. 'They may not have been singled out for discrimination and not marked out for special favours in the last ten years. But as far as Muslims are concerned in Gujarat or anywhere else in the country, Modi is not, and cannot ever be the preferred choice. This is the truth,' says Zia Ur Rahman, a doctor based in Kolkata.

J.S. Bandukwala, former professor of Physics at the Maharaja Sayaji University (MSU) in Vadodara and himself a riot victim in 2002, says that Modi's prime ministerial ambitions are cause for Muslims all across the country to get alert and foil the attempt electorally. He especially points at eastern states like Bihar, UP, Assam, and West Bengal, where Muslims comprise over 20 per cent of the population. He believes that communal polarization cannot happen in these states as easily as it did in Gujarat. 'A leopard does not change its spots. To think that we will have a new Modi in love with the Muslims is an illusion that we should get rid of,' says Teesta

Setalvad, who has been fighting the Modi regime for the last ten years. Incidentally, in his hate speech MIM's Akbaruddin Owaisi had also asserted: 'that we will never allow Modi who has killed 2000 Muslims to be *wazir-e-azam* (prime minister).' Owaisi was sent to jail but now has a bigger fan following among Muslims for his anti-Modi statements.

In the ultimate analysis, the Sadbhavana efforts of Modi may not have yielded anything substantial for the man eyeing the top slot in Delhi. For the average Muslim, he is still a Hindutva icon.

9

Modi: The Man

In most respects, Gujarat is a very modern state. But in the matter of allowing consumption of liquor at hotels and parties, the otherwise forward-looking state has remained obstructionist. Ask anyone over the age of fifty and he will tell you about the merits of prohibition: about how women are safe moving around at night, because there are no drunkards on the road, about how the law-and-order scenario is not marred because of this, etc. In reality, this is a hypocritical situation because booze flows freely in Gujarat. Though there may not be liquor shops around where you can crowd to pick up your bottle or pouch, there are friendly neighbourhood agents just a phone call away. They will send the stuff to your home, no questions asked. In many other states, taxes levied on liquor sales generate huge revenues but in the otherwise practical Gujarat, nobody is willing to bell the cat.

Prohibition in Gujarat is the gift of Mahatma Gandhi and has been in vogue since the state was formed in 1960. In the first few decades, the state was ruled by the Congress whose chief ministers had to follow the Gandhian diktats. But this is a status quo that has not changed under the BJP raj and even during Modi's tenure. Meanwhile in the last fifteen years, state governments have been under great pressure from the industrial lobby for lifting prohibition on the grounds that it hindered flow of investments especially in sectors like information technology. But to no avail. The irony is that even a bold administrator like Modi, has not been able to summon the requisite courage to stand up and say – in the words of a business baron: 'Folks, prohibition is an anachronism – let's get rid of it.'

Interestingly, Modi realizes that prohibition has outlived its utility and many like me swear that in private conversations, he admits as much. 'Modi is an iconoclast but only so long as he perceives that the destruction of this icon – the ban on liquor – will not recoil on him. If he thinks it will, Modi will back off. To that extent he is extremely practical,' asserts a politician who knows him well. He is obviously not willing to take a risk and would be content with a few relaxations here and there. Many believe that the crime rate in Gujarat is low because the police makes all their moolah by turning a Nelson's eye at illegal liquor trade and are therefore in a position to clamp down on other crimes. Modi's views on the subject are not known, but he has obviously not been able to summon the courage to dismiss this anachronism.

In a rather inverse example of Modi's practical nature, the politician quoted above also says that this Gujarat 'hriday samrat' would have clamped down on the riots of 2002 with an iron hand if he had perceived that persistence of a law-and-order breakdown would leave him with egg on his face in the ensuing elections. 'But Modi knew that he had popular support in his own state and this was proven by the results of the year-end elections. He is a great one for gauging public mood. In that sense, he is like water which takes the shape of the container into which it is poured. But he gives a contrary impression of being bold and decisive. This is not always the case,' says the politician. He also speculates that Modi, who has not apologized to the Muslims for the riots of 2002, will do so the moment he realizes that the political capital he could garner from this good will would outweigh anything else.

Modi's knack for gauging public mood is attributed to his days in the RSS, where he was trained as an organizer. Like all organizers, he was groomed to speak and listen to a huge number of people and gather information. 'I am half a newsman,' remarked Modi when I entered his chief ministerial office one day, many years ago. Modi was reading reams of papers on his table: print-outs of freshly-filed stories on the newswires. 'The way he gossips is not funny. A lot of his conversation relates to people. This must be his way to collect information. He uses the information to assess a situation or a person and for formulating strategy,' says a journalist who knows him well. 'He can be a newsman's delight or nightmare, depending on which way you look at it,' says another reporter. His reason: Modi makes it a point to read and scrutinize newspapers and websites and react to the stories almost immediately. Most other contemporaries of Modi across the nation are not known to be so alert and on the ball. 'Modiji has a wonderful memory and has no difficulty remembering people he may have met years ago. He is able to connect with people by remembering their personal details,' says Jai Narain Vyas who served in the Modi cabinet between 2007-12.

This reliance on gathering of information has also helped Modi develop another skill: that of public relations which, in some ways, is a related trade. 'Modi's skills are not merely for gathering news but also for packaging and disseminating this information,' says a senior IAS officer of Gujarat who has seen him from close quarters. 'He is a master spin-doctor and uses information to create a larger-than-life image of himself,' the officer adds. A good example of this is the 3D technology that Modi leveraged in the last election to deliver speeches. 'We used the technology to beam 3D hologram images of Modi delivering his election speeches to up to 52 different places. To viewers, it looked as though the real Modi had stepped out to walk and talk,' said film director Mani Shankar from Hyderabad, who imported the technology from the UK, where it is used to beam music shows. 'We did not approach Mr Modi with our services. His men sought us out,' Mani Shankar shared. The film director also reveals that Modi was dressed differently each day for the 3D show:

in an array of multi-coloured kurtas. A public relations specialist says that Modi seems to believe in the dictum that 'style is the man.' He is well-groomed, wears good clothes, dons Ray-Ban sunglasses and shows off pedicured feet with clipped nails and scrubbed skin.

Those who know him well say that he has been fond of good attire and personal grooming from the very beginning. 'He came from a very small town where most people did not iron their clothes. Modi, as a boy, thus had no access to ironing services. But he would try to press his clothes by using some heavy objects or whatever best he could lay his hands on,' says journalist Darshan Desai who has researched his early days. RSS insiders remember how he ran afoul of his bosses in his early days in the organization, when he trimmed his beard in order to look better. This apparently was not the norm in the RSS, at least then.

In the early '80s he started patronizing a barber – a Muslim incidentally – who had his salon close to the RSS headquarters and who gave him a Rajesh Khanna style haircut. A few years later, Modi started riding a Bajaj Chetak scooter. Particular about his clothes, after becoming chief minister, he began patronizing Jade Blue, a clothing outfit in Ahmedabad that has outlets outside Gujarat too. Tailors from Jade Blue reportedly go to his house and take his measurements. The shop has now developed its own brand of Modi kurtas.

If stylish clothes go a long way in enhancing the personality, so do pictures. Modi knows this very well. If those who have had a peep at his portfolio are to be believed, it contains hundreds of shots of the big man striking various poses. Modi also loves to project himself as a hero, a powerful man, destroying all villains. Any contra-projection angers him. I got a taste of this on the morrow of the Akshardham incident in September 2002. When the *Times of India* reported how Modi and Advani ventured to enter the complex and pose next to the bodies of the two assailants who had been shot to death, I was greeted by an early morning call from an incensed Modi. 'Why are you writing that we went in after the intruders were killed? It conveys that I am a weak man,' Modi said.

Analysts who have seen him from close, agree that Modi loves his image of an Alpha-Male. 'He is especially the subject of adulation amongst women. Many well-educated, well-heeled women swoon over him. Many are head-over-heels in love with him, without knowing him personally,' confirm observers. 'Gujarat is essentially a mercantile state with no martial tradition. So heroes of the Bollywood type, successful in doing the impossible are conspicuous by their absence in Gujarat. But perhaps there is a perceived need for such heroes in the state, especially amongst women. The image of Modi satiates that need,' speculates Reema Desai, a forty-year-old Gujarati woman who lives in Mumbai. However, many journalists on the Modi trail in the last elections confirm that this adulation amongst women is waning.

'Mahatma Gandhi with his practice of austerity, abstinence and tremendous self-control became the hero of Gujarat in earlier days. But now, we Gujaratis want a hero like Modi and – he is on offer,' Desai says. In other words, much of his machismo is on display, only because people love it.

Journalists like Sheela Bhatt believe (though these views do not have many takers) that when riots broke out after the Godhra carnage, Modi 'got damn scared' but persisted with (ill-advised) bravado. Two days into the riots and when asked about the Gulberg Society episode, where former Congress MP Ehsan Jafri was killed, Modi said that every 'kriya had a pratikriya' (the action of Godhra has had a reaction). To the rest of the nation, such a statement was shocking. But Modi was brazen because he felt that his constituents in Gujarat loved it.

Modi-watchers aver that he pursues a policy of selective brinkmanship. They recall the story of Haren Pandya, the upcoming BJP leader from Gujarat, who could have emerged as a threat to Modi's political position. Modi first dropped him from the ministry (he was revenue minister) and then sought to deny him a seat for the 2002 assembly elections though he was a sitting MLA. Leaders like Advani and Jaitely intervened on Pandya's behalf but to dodge pressure, Modi got admitted to the hospital. A few days later when the pressure showed no signs of abating, Modi declared that he would not contest the elections, if a ticket was given to Pandya. Both Advani and Jaitely backed off, leaving Pandya out in the cold. A few months later, Pandya was murdered outside a public park in unclear circumstances. A CBI case was thrown out of high court and the accused was let off. Both, Pandya's father and wife have termed the murder as 'political,' leaving no doubt about what they believe. But this was one murder that shell-shocked and created a negative image in the minds of the terrified Gujaratis.

Weaving fantasies and singing paeans to the glory of their favourite hero is also part of the Modi myth. Many in Gujarat who participated in the Navnirman movement of 1974 say that Modi fans try to project him as the hero of the movement, when he did not even have a role in the affair. They also say that it is ludicrous to suggest that Loknayak Jayaprakash Narayan was impressed by what he saw of Modi in those days. 'This is absolute balderdash,' says social activist Hanif Lakdawala. 'I am not too sure that JP even encountered Modi.'

'Wonder if such myth-making has the support of Modi,' says another student leader of those days. He points out how these cries of 'dekho dekho koun aya, Gujarat ka sher aya' which greets Modi at election meetings, may not be all that spontaneous. Even Modi's men do not deny that their boss has the knack for creating hype.

Everybody agrees that Modi is a good orator and an effective public speaker. Part of this ability is God-given and part developed by training in the RSS, which places a lot of emphasis on the ability to communicate. But almost everybody agrees that Modi hits opponents below the belt and resorts to cheap humour that titillates, but is not expected of a person so high in public life. 'To that extent, he has not overgrown his mofussil days. Such cheap diatribes are lapped up by rural crowds,' says a minister in his government. A TV anchor however, says that Modi used to be crude on the box before he became chief minister. 'He was ready for a fight and often his facial expressions put off many viewers,' he says. All through Elections 2012, he referred to Prime Minister Manmohan Singh as '*Moun*' Mohan Singh alluding to the silence he maintained on many public matters. 'This is the sort of stuff that goes around in SMS jokes, not fit to be part of a speech of a leader,' says Paranjoy Guha Thakurta. The recent instance of Modi labeling Sunanda Puskhar as the '₹50 crore wife' of Congressman Shashi Tharoor, also indicates the Modi brand of humour (Tharoor's repartee was that his wife was priceless). I also recollect how I too was the butt of this cheap humour in the midst of the 2002 riots. A phone call was received by a colleague from an inspector of the Intelligence branch, who informed her that there was a threat of physical attack upon me. I immediately called up the chief secretary and director-general of police, who were nonplussed and seemed to be ignorant of the threat. A little while later, Modi called me up himself and guffawed: 'What is all this that I am hearing about a life threat to you? Arrey, I only told the Intelligence to ensure your safety. After all, you are writing so much against the police, that I thought that somebody could attack you.'

Analysts think that Modi excels in an adversarial role: where there is a foe to vanquish. That is why he always requires an enemy. The enemy for him is the (pseudo) secular establishment, Nehruvian traditions, and the liberal press. Portraying them as the 'ruling establishment' responsible for all the ills in the country, he takes on a revolutionary role, seeking to destroy them. The fact that he had a lean frame and sported a black beard like revolutionaries of yore has helped attract the attention of change-seekers. Even though Modi now has a white beard, broad frame and has been in power for ten years, he is still able to don the image of a revolutionary by declaring that his mission is to change the status quo of fifty years. He declares that the ten years he has been in power has been spent *like a revolutionary* fighting these well-rooted forces of 'no change.'

But Modi is no fool: the good old enemy, Pakistan is always handy. In the 2007 election campaign, he talked about Mian Musharraf as if his battle was against the then Pakistani president. In the 2012 elections, he raised irrelevant issues such as the Sir Creek dispute with Pakistan and upped the ante the moment visiting Pakistani interior minister Rehman Malik raised the issue of the demolition of Babri Masjid and labelled terrorist Abu Jundal as an agent of Indian Intelligence.

Modi is a master strategist. 'It is not an easy thing to win three straight elections. Modi won Elections 2012 by intelligently pitching it as a direct battle between himself and the Central government in Delhi. Thus when the voter was making his decision, in his mind it was a choice between Modi and a candidate who belonged to a party responsible for major scandals in the country in the last two years. This is how he overcame the anti-incumbency of being in power for ten years,' says corporate consultant Sunil Parekh.

Acutely aware that many BJP candidates could attract significant anti-incumbency, Modi exhorted voters to assume he was the candidate in all the constituencies and thus not evaluate the candidate and cast their votes.

It is a result of this strategy that Modi has been able to reinforce the image that 'Modi is Gujarat and Gujarat is Modi' and that if you attack Modi, you attack the entire Gujarati community. 'This has been skillfully evoked by invoking "Gujarati Asmita" (self-pride of Gujaratis) and I am sure that hours and hours of deep thinking must have gone into this. He is a highly-focused man and knows exactly what he wants. It was Mahatma Gandhi's belief that the means were more important to achieve the ends; Modi turns the dictum around,' says a public relations expert.

'He is well versed in Chanakya niti and the techniques of *saam, daam, dand, bhed* (equality, enticement, punishment, and sowing dissension) and uses them to good effect. He maintains dossiers on who he perceives are potential trouble makers,' confides an officer, who had earlier served in his intelligence set-up. But the official admits that misusing the intelligence set-up is not something that is restricted to Modi. 'All top politicians in power do this,' he says.

I remember how in 2002, I was advised by an Intelligence official to change my cell number, because Modi sahib had ordered for 'daily print outs' of my cell conversations. Though I could not authenticate the veracity of the claim made by the officer, but had no reason to disbelieve him either.

Those most skeptical of Modi and his ways, however, agree that under his rule, petty bureaucratic corruption has been reduced. 'We do business in many states but in Gujarat we do not find the kind of corruption at babu level that we find in other states,' says Shyamlal Patnaik, representative of Du Pont, an MNC.

Bureaucrats in Gujarat however, say that corruption has not been reduced in the state, only, that it has become 'subtle', with the number of participants shrinking. Analysts point out that with the objective of reducing the political class to ciphers, Modi has started dealing directly with bureaucrats. The latter are also happy to do his bidding because they have now only one boss – the top man himself, to deal with.

But true to his nature of not pushing the envelope too much lest it rock his boat, Modi repeated most MLAs as candidates for the 2012 election, knowing full well that many of them were highly unpopular. This is due to the sudden entry of Keshubhai Patel into the elections as the third front. The Modi dispensation has also co-opted local-level sarpanchs and political executives with allegiance to the Congress into the bigger BJP game plan by intelligently instilling into them – weird though this may seem – the notion that working for Modi in the state and Sonia in the Centre, is not something inconsistent with each other.

'Modi is a full-time and consummate politician. Every waking moment of his day is spent thinking and strategizing power play,' says one of his ministers.

Considering his modest background, Modi has come a long way in life. The credit for his persistence and determination cannot be taken away from him, concede even his worst critics. 'If you look at his horoscope, he certainly must be having "neecha bhanga" yog, which enables people born low-down in society to reach the absolute top by dint of their own merit,' says the minister quoted above.

But in this process of ascent, Modi has metamorphosed. With such a mofussil background, Modi would have been expected to be the darling of the rural masses. But today, Modi is more popular in urban areas than in villages, even as a great urban-rural divide is becoming increasingly visible in Gujarat.

For all the adulation that Modi draws in the public space, he has no friends or family. Though his mother and brother, too, live in Gandhinagar, he resides alone. It is an open secret that Modi has nothing to do with his siblings and even visits his mother rarely. One of these occasions is on his birthday, on 17 September, when he goes to seek the blessings of Heeraba, his nearly ninety-year-old mother.

But the nastier of his critics say that this is more for the photo opportunity that it provides. In spite of her frail health, Heeraba cast her vote during the recent elections. Modi is the third child of six children. The brother Pankaj with whom his mother stays, is a junior official – a group B officer in the information department of the Gujarat government. He goes to work at the same Sachivalaya where his elder brother is the top boss. An elder brother of Modi – with whom his mother lived earlier – also stays in Ahmedabad and runs a fair price shop. Newshounds recollect how Modi's mother had come for his swearing-in in 2001 and stood in a corner, till someone recognized her and offered a chair. An admirer of Modi says that he believes in the dictum that kingship knows no kinship, and that the efficiency of his government is due to the fact that he has no children or nephews to indulge in deal-making, as is usually the case. 'He has no funds stashed away in Swiss banks. At a time when fingers are being pointed at almost every other neta, Modi stands tall. Nobody seems to recognize this,' says Narottam Shah, a businessman.

Among his ministers he is friendly only with his old political associate, Anandiben Patel and industry minister, Saurabh Patel, who also happens to be the son-in-law of Ramnikbhai Ambani, the elder brother of Dhirubhai Ambani. Modi was believed to be close to his former home minister, Amit Shah, who was later excommunicated from Gujarat for many months on court orders, after being released on bail. Shah had been arrested in connection with the Sohrabuddin Sheikh fake encounter case. After being excommunicated, Shah lived in Delhi at the state government-run Gujarat Bhavan and accompanied Modi to the dais at a BJP national executive meeting in Suraj Kund. He stood for elections in 2012 and was re-elected.

Modi is also believed to be close to first-generation industrialist, Gautam Adani, who runs a port and a successful import-export business, besides owning coal-mining rights in Australia. Adani is very active in propagating the Modi image abroad along with a bevy of Gujarat businessmen. Bureaucrats like K. Kailashnathan, Modi's principal secretary for long and Maheswar Sahu, principal secretary in charge of industry have been doing his bidding for many years and are his trusted aides. So is his secretary, A.K. Sharma, who has been with him for a decade. Jagatheesa Pandian, principal secretary in the energy department is also a Modi man. He was earlier private secretary to P. Chidambaram in Delhi. Even Sahu, who looks after the Vibrant Gujarat show, was private secretary to Murasoli Maran, then commerce minister of India. Parendu Bhagat, a middle-level BJP member who does odd jobs for Modi is reputedly close to him. His son, Maulik Bhagat is in charge of Modi's forays in cyber space. 'It appears that Modi has numerous professionals managing his image, but I don't know who they are,' a Modi minister says.

Those who know him well say that Modi follows a system of reward and punishment and whatever he does is with a purpose. But they say that he has 'forgotten' many who did him a good turn in his early days. For instance, a RSS leader Vishnu Pandya, who edited the mouthpiece of the organization in Gujarat titled *Sadhana*, is known to have provided tutelage to Modi in his salad days. But if insiders are to be believed, the two are not even on talking terms now.

A bureaucrat (in service till recently) recollects how he had to plead with Modi for a promotion that had been due to him for six months, before it was effected.

'Even for things that you deserve, Modi makes you feel that he is doing a great favour,' says this officer. But when it suits Modi's purpose, he also supersedes other officers to promote a particular one, even if the beneficiary of the generosity may not otherwise, be a favourite. A good example is the promotion of P.K. Laheri, as chief secretary of the state in 2003. Though a competent officer, Laheri superseded many officers just because he was a son-of-the-soil. 'In those days Modi was promoting Gujarati Asmita in a big way and felt that appointing a Gujarati chief secretary would send an effective message,' says an officer who witnessed the process from close quarters.

Not unusual for a leader from a Hindu right-wing party, Modi is a fervent believer in gods and goddesses. He is a *bhakta* of Ma Durga and observes a dawn-to-late night fast for nine days every Navaratri, partaking only of fruits at the end of the day. I remember Modi calling me during Navaratris and expressing a desire to visit the Durga puja organized by the Bengali community in Gandhinagar. Temple-hopping forms part of his political yatras, which often start from and conclude at a temple. For instance, his election campaign for 2012 started from the Somnath temple, while his Sadbhavna Yatra ended at the Ambaji temple. His recent Vivekananda Yuva Yatra also started from the holy town of Becharji 'with the blessings of Bhahuchar Mata' (to quote Modi). Becharji is a *shakti peetha*, where the hand of Sati fell when Lord Shiva, angered by her suicide, threw her body. (According to mythology, Sati was the first wife of Shiva. Unable to bear the humiliation meted out by her father to Shiva, she gave up her life). The other *shakti peethas* in Gujarat are in Ambaji and Pavagadh in central Gujarat. But of the three, Becharji, being in his home district of Mehsana and probably one he was exposed to early in life, is a favourite with Modi.

The most mysterious aspect of his life relates to his supposed marriage to Jashodaben Chimanlal, which he does not talk about.

Many journalists like Darshan Desai had met Jashodaben in 2002 in north Gujarat, where she worked as a primary school teacher. This was obviously to Modi's chagrin, because Desai got a call from the big man the moment he returned from the trip.

'Modi wanted to know what I was up to,' recalls Desai, to whom the lady had confirmed her marriage to Modi. Before the 2007 elections, a clipping of Jashodaben had appeared on YouTube, wherein she related the story of her marriage and how she was still waiting for Modi.

Before the 2012 elections some intrepid reporters once again made a beeline for Jashodaben's village hoping for fresh news bytes. But she could not be found in spite of their best efforts. Villagers said that she had retired from her job and moved on.

Modi is not only extremely dogged but also very hard-working, often at the cost of his health. Newspaper reports from Gujarat about the 2012 election campaign reveal that Modi maintained a punishing schedule in spite of persistent backaches, swollen legs and a sore throat. The sore throat is reported to have really bothered him after the first phase of elections that ended on 14 December and Modi had to seek medical attention to ensure that his vocal cords were intact for campaigning in the next few days. The *Times of India* reported that he was one-man-army, a man possessed, addressing an average of 19 meetings a day, other than his 3D appearances, in the course of 15 days. This election campaign schedule was preceded by a month-long Vivekananda Yuva Vikas Yatra which was used by Modi as a warm-up to the actual election campaign. But even during these warm-up sessions, Modi addressed 135 rallies in the course of a month. The *Times of India* computed that as a result of the yatra and election campaigning schedule, Modi was able to touch all the 182 assembly seats twice over. The invocation of the name Vivekananda for the yatra demonstrates how inventive Modi is. Besides this year being the 150th birth anniversary of Swami Vivekananda (which meant that the yatra was dove-tailed onto a series of events across the country to commemorate the occasion) Modi drew a parallel between himself and Swamiji, because he was a Hindu monk and a brahmachari too. More interestingly, Vivekananda's original name was Narendra Nath Dutta. Modi calculated that this would bring up an invariable comparison with his own first name and in public perception, hopefully transfer some of the sterling qualities of Vivekananda to Modi.

As Modi himself wrote in a blog, he chose 11 September to kick-start his yatra because this was the day in 1893 when Swami Vivekananda addressed the World Congress of Religions in Chicago. Of course, he did not fail to also note that these days, 9/11 brought to mind the destructive pictures of aeroplanes crashing into the Twin Towers in New York, but that he would rather remember the speech of Swamiji.

Tech-savvy Modi writes a blog on the *Times of India* site and is off-the-mark very quickly. Barely 45 minutes after the final round of polling for the 2012 elections was over at 5 pm on 17 December, Modi's blog titled 'Historic turnout at the polls, congrats to the people of Gujarat' was up. Two days earlier after the first phase of elections, Modi had blogged about the marvels of 3D technology that he 'proudly' used to communicate his message. He added: 'Technology is the medium. The bond that I share with the people is that of the heart and runs very deep.'

Those who read his blogs say that he tries to portray himself not only as a man of the masses, but also as a self-effacing one. '*Main nahin hum*' (not I but we), is what he stresses in his blog writings though, in reality, this is not what his personality is all about. He wrote a blog on his birthday, in which he said that his birthday was a day like any other and every day was special to him. In his blog, Modi also projects himself as the 'common man' (CM) and not chief minister (CM), preferring to describe himself as a 'practical dreamer' who has the ability to convert dreams into reality.

Besides being a blogger, Modi is also on Twitter and his men claim that he has half-a-million followers. But this is a grossly exaggerated figure, say cyber experts who have examined this claim. For the 2012 elections, Modi also relied on a newly-started Internet TV channel called NaMo, to spread his message.

Though Modi may be naturally inclined towards modern gadgets, his harnessing of technology is also part of strategy to overhaul his image of Hindutva. 'A technology-savvy man is a forward-looking man, while Hindutva is rooted in the mores of a medieval man. Modi is trying to make a leap through harnessing technology and this is why he makes a big deal of it', says Rahul Sharma, president of a public affairs firm, Genesis. He also knows how to use TV effectively. Those who have observed him closely, point at how, in the course of an election rally, he switches from Gujarati to Hindi the minute he sees cameras of national channels.

In order to appear 'cool' and as the first Indian politician to chat 'live' with netizens, Modi also appeared on Google+ chat in late August 2012.

The chat was broadcast live on YouTube. But the fact that questions had to be submitted ahead, took the sting out of a 'live' chat. Questions related to subjects like education, youth empowerment, urbanization issues, and rural development. A day before the session, Modi tweeted: 'Friends I am looking forward to exchanging ideas with you on G+ hangout tomorrow and on realizing Swami Vivekananda's vision of strong India.' Analysts, however, call this 'show-baazi' and say that if he were so 'cool', he should have had a real live chat. The chat was moderated by film star, Ajay Devgan. Many say that Modi wants to draw a glamour quotient from cine artists: it is not without reason that Modi has hired Amitabh Bachchan as the tourism ambassador for Gujarat. Actor-turned-businesswoman, Preity Zinta, too, is invited to Vibrant Gujarat. With the same idea in mind, Olympic medalist, Gagan Narang was encouraged to call on Modi to seek land to establish a shooting academy in Gandhinagar.

Image consultants analyze that since Modi may be up against Rahul Gandhi for the PM's post in the next general election, this emphasis in appearing to be youthful is aimed at beating competition. But cold and calculative though he is, Modi also wants to project himself as a sensitive man. To that end, he wrote an anthology of poems titled *Ankh A Dhanya Che* (Blessed Are These Eyes) in 2007. But most who have read the book say that the quality of the poetry is, at best, pedestrian and only provides an insight into the 'I, Me and Mine' philosophy of the man. He also has some books to his credit, including one called *Sangharsha Ma Gujarat* that relates to the situation of Gujarat during the Emergency, which was not reported in popular media because of censorship in the press. However, the book does not seem to have sold well. In recent years, some of his speeches and thoughts have been compiled into books by the Gujarat government including *Karmayog*, a compilation of his lectures to bureaucrats at a *Chintin Shibir* he organized.

An ambitious man has to be a great survivor as well. For self-preservation, Modi can go to any lengths to rabble-rouse. In 2010, before he had to appear before the special investigations team (SIT) set up by the Supreme Court to investigate the 2002 riots, Modi published on his website 'a letter to my countrymen' where he tried to raise the temperature by accusing 'a nexus amongst the vested interests in spreading lies. The machination has come unstuck, for people have seen through this charade.' At another level, Modi's survival instincts were seen at their best in the interregnum between the completion of polling on 17 December and announcement of results on 20 December.

Not one to rest, Modi was engaged in deep confabulation with aides trying to identify 'winnable' candidates from small parties who could be lured into BJP, in case the party failed to get a solid majority on its own. In the event he won a comfortable victory and thus the meetings were unnecessary.

But then: is Modi a man to leave anything to chance?

IO

The Chinese Connection

Vested with the responsibility of maintaining relations with external powers, it is not unusual for sovereign governments to skew their foreign policy in favour of select countries. But, for a state government with no responsibility whatsoever to engage with foreign powers to devise a 'look east' foreign policy, could look a trifle surprising. For the record, Narendra Modi did not ever say that his Gujarat government has a 'look east' policy. But those keeping close tabs on him know that ever since his prime ministerial ambitions grew post-2009, Modi has been crafting a policy of engaging with China and Japan at the cost of the US and UK.

In some senses this has been thrust on Modi: both the US and the UK have denied him a visa because of his poor human rights record. Modi, always defiant in the face of opposition, decided that he would take on the US and UK by trying to warm up to China and Japan.

A culmination of these efforts was seen in the Vibrant Gujarat 2013 show which witnessed a red carpet laid out for the Chinese, who participated in the show for the first time. The Japanese participants at the show who had attended earlier shows were present in strength.

However, with Modi winning again in 2012 and perceived to be making a bid for New Delhi in the near future, the US and UK may also change their policies towards him.

Evidence of the changing international position on Modi became clear on 8 February when the German ambassador to India, Michael Steiner, indicated that the European Union was lifting the informal ten-year ban on Modi. Steiner disclosed that Modi had lunch with EU ambassadors in Delhi last month, during which Modi reportedly said that the 2002 riots were unfortunate and promised that there would be no recurrence. Modi reportedly also said the right things about inclusiveness at the lunch meeting. Later, Modi disclosed on his own blog that he has been invited to attend the EU Parliament in November this year in Brussels.

'For China – which has ethnic minorities in Tibet and Xinjiang – and given the Tiannanmen Square episode and its own indifferent human rights record, Gujarat 2002 is no issue at all. The Chinese do not have a liberal press and human rights lobby that would question the government. When Modi realized this, he began to assiduously court the Chinese,' admits a senior official of the Gujarat government.

'The Tiannanmen Square riots made China an international pariah. But Deng Xiaoping turned the tide by unleashing economic reforms. This made the Chinese a favourite with the international business community. Comparison – between Gujarat and China – may not be exactly in order but that's roughly what Modi has been trying to do,' says Ajit Rangnekar, Dean of Indian School of Business, who has watched China very closely for the last three decades. Others think that Modi, with his authoritarian streak was inspired by the Chinese model to script a similar story with rapid growth and visible development that held the rest of the world in awe.

The fact that China was fast emerging as numero uno trading partner for India helped Modi observe the superpower. Indo–Chinese trade grew from US $43.28 billion in 2009 to US $73.90 billion in 2011.

'In the good old days, fans of China used to be found in the ranks of the Communist party and among students in Indian universities, points out V. Venkataramana, professor of management at the University of Hyderabad. 'But with China pursuing open door policies, all top Indian companies are doing business in China. India–China friendship societies, too, are mushrooming in all cities.'

Many companies from Gujarat including Reliance, Essar, and Adanis do big business with China. For instance, Essar has been importing machinery worth billions of dollars from China for its steel, telecom, energy, and power businesses for the last few years. The Adani group, whose promoters are reputedly very close to Modi, has in fact been employing technicians – about 3000 – from China, to commission a power plant in Mundhra in Gujarat's Kutch district. Of course, the equipment for the power plant, too, is of Chinese manufacture. Adanis have also initiated coal supply agreements with Chinese companies. Over the first decade of the twenty-first century, many Gujarati traders started frequenting Shanghai and other parts of China for business. Even tourist traffic of Gujaratis seeking an exotic holiday in China has increased.

The involvement of these companies helped Modi take a decision to hitch his wagon to that of the Chinese. The first sign of the initiative came in late August 2011, when the India China Economic and Cultural Council's (ICEC) Gujarat chapter was opened in Ahmedabad. The occasion was used by the Chinese ambassador to travel down to Gujarat and invite Narendra Modi to China. This was followed by a trip by the Chinese vice-minister of 'international development' of the CPC, Ai Ping to Ahmedabad. He, too, extended an invitation to Modi.

Modi was quick to capitalize on the invites. Just three months later – in November 2011 – with a delegation of Gujarat businessmen in tow, he landed in China.

According to the India China Economic and Cultural Council, both the government of the Peoples' Republic of China and the ruling Communist Party of China (CPC) 'accorded unprecedented importance and highest level of protocol' to Modi, 'going beyond established norms.' Special arrangements were made for receptions, banquets, visits, security, and high-level meetings

But there was a far more important feature to the visit: Narendra Modi was received at the Great Hall of People in Beijing, where heads of states of national government are normally received. A meeting was also organized with Wang Gang, vice chairman of the China Peoples' Consultative Conference and member of the politbureau of the Chinese Communist party. So it was not only Modi courting the Chinese – the reverse was also the case.

Modi, with his uncanny eye for detail, printed his card in Mandarin and in red, to show his seriousness about the trip. The first two characters used to write his name in Mandarin are the same as for Nalan Xingde, a seventeenth-century Qing dynasty poet who died young but is still popular in China.

During his trip, Modi and his delegation sold the story that Gujarat could be a window of opportunity for the Chinese, because of the state's 1650 kilometre long coastline. Further, Gujarat provided easy access to the Middle East, European and African markets for Chinese companies operating in the state. Doing so would also help these companies reduce costs, especially at a time that Chinese corporations were moving inland and away from their coastal bases. This was to cope with rising costs due to rising rents and power tariffs. An MoU was also signed with Sichuan province, an inland state in China, that has not yet seen as much development as the eastern ocean springboard has.

Apparently, while signing the MoU, Modi's men were told that in contrast to their earlier policies of only developing exports, the new Chinese policy is also to develop internal markets. Sichuan province was one of the states where this was proposed and hence this engagement with Gujarat.

Besides matters of trade and growing business relationships among the two countries, Modi raised the issue of twenty-two Gujarati traders languishing in Chinese jails for over a year without a trial. They had been arrested by customs at Shenzhen for (allegedly)

smuggling 'diamonds into China from Hong Kong.' According to Modi's blog, his 'diplomatic efforts and statesmanship' showed results and the twenty-two diamond traders got 'relief'. Thirteen of these traders – mostly from Surat and Mumbai – were freed and the remaining sentenced to jail terms (which brought predictability in their life, because they know how long they would be in prison and also that they will not be held indefinitely in jail).

Modi also raised the issue of Chinese presence in Pakistan Occupied Kashmir (POK) and said that Pakistan was 'using' China. Modi also stated that being a border state that had borne hostility from Pakistan, Gujarat, too, was apprehensive about that country. He also pointed out to the wrong map of Arunachal Pradesh as depicted by China. It is obvious that these contentions had little effect on the Chinese, who merely heard Modi's arguments out.

'China is interested only in China. If it feels that courting Modi is in the interest of China, it will do so,' says a senior diplomat who is serving as India's ambassador to a south-east Asian country. He adds that the reception of Modi had much to do with a 'message that the Chinese were seeking to convey at that time to the Congress party which heads the government in Delhi.'

The diplomat, however, agrees that the Chinese possibly reckon that Modi will be an important national political figure and therefore see merit in courting him. 'China makes a clear distinction between short-term and long-term interests. If it suits them to court him, they will do so. If it suits them to drop him, they will do so too,' the diplomat says. With Modi's rise beyond the boundaries of Gujarat, it is obviously in China's interest to buttress their advantage by courting him before other countries do. A slightly skeptical minister in Modi's government felt that the Chinese government will not go out of the way to root for Modi. 'I do not think that any sovereign government can have a particular policy towards a state government. Their policy towards Gujarat will be the same as their policy towards India,' the minister said.

Incidentally, Bihar chief minister, Nitish Kumar, who is seen as Modi's bête noire, had visited China a few months before the Gujarat counterpart, but was unable to generate the sort of interest that the latter's trip did.

Modi's visit was followed by that of other Gujarat delegations, including road shows – in Beijing, Shanghai, Chengdu, Guangzhou and Hong Kong – seeking participation from that country in Vibrant Gujarat 2013.

Representatives of many Chinese companies have also visited the Indian state, after Modi declared that Gujarat was open for business with them.

Some deals have also been signed. This includes a deal between the Torrent group and a Chinese company to market drugs of the latter in India. A Chinese company is investing $452 million to establish a facility to manufacture transformers in Vadodara. Also being developed is a green energy park. A Government of Gujarat official says that the state is targeting at least 10 per cent of the $100 billion Chinese investment being planned in India. The Dholera special investment region – off the Delhi–Mumbai Industrial corridor – is being promoted massively to the Chinese. The region is also being similarly pushed to the Japanese.

In order to deepen the engagement between China and Gujarat, two universities in Gujarat have also readied plans to offer Mandarin language courses. In reciprocation, Beijing University too is planning to teach Gujarati. This would be the second Indian language after Hindi that the university will offer.

Modi's dalliance with China, however, has drawn flak. The Sangh parivar, to which Modi owes his allegiance, has other ideas about China. With China propping up Pakistan militarily, economically, and in other ways, elements in the Sangh parivar almost equate China with Pakistan, as perceived enemies of India. They are also extremely annoyed that the Indian nation is being challenged by the Chinese, who show Arunachal Pradesh as part of China and refuse to issue visas to residents of the state with the provocative claim that since China is their own country, Arunachalis do not require a visa.

China is also seen as using Nepal to foment trouble in India. 'As India's external affairs minister in Morarji Desai's government, Vajpayee too, had tried to mend relations with neighbours. Even then, Modi's inclination towards China is not expected to satisfy his hard-core colleagues,' says a Gujarat MLA.

More importantly, Sichuan province with which Gujarat is developing special economic relations, is part of extended Tibet and inhabited by a lot of Buddhists. In the last two years, many young Buddhists have immolated themselves in protest against the continuous occupation of Tibet by the Chinese and intensified efforts to totally annihilate the Tibetan culture. In fact most Tibetan self-immolations have taken place in this province. The Chinese government has been claiming that these suicides were spurred on by activities of outside agencies like the Dalai Lama's government-in-exile. They have been trying to prevail upon the Indian government to rein in the Dalai Lama, but to no effect. In fact in 2011, the Chinese called off border talks with India, after the Government of India refused to clamp down on the Dalai Lama.

'Traditionally the BJP has been critical of GOI for going soft on Tibet and not supporting the legitimate aspirations of the Tibetan people. How, then, can a possible BJP government with Modi at the helm, be critical of the Chinese with such extensive business relations?' asked an Indian foreign service officer.

Incidentally most of the Chinese exports to India are finished products and include furniture, fertilizers and a host of other items. But Indian exports to China are raw materials like iron ore, cotton yarn, leather, salt, and sulphur. Of this, iron ore is the most prominent and till 2011 it accounted for more than half of Indian exports. The iron ore is used by the Chinese steel manufacturers as raw material and the steel produced is used to build infrastructure. The balance of trade is skewed heavily against India. The gap between Indian imports and exports to China is rising: from US $15.87 billion in 2009 it increased to US $27.08 billion in 2011. Indian exports to China face strong non-tariff barriers but the reverse is the case.

'The Indian market is flooded with Chinese goods. Even small things like safety pins are being sent by the Chinese to India. They are eroding our competitiveness. And yet, we have not blocked Chinese imports,' points out a top businessman. 'The pattern of trade between India and China is similar to that between a developed country (which manufactures finished products) and its satellite (that supplies raw materials). I do not know how long is it possible for India to maintain such an adverse balance of trade with a country like China that is by no means a friend of India. More pertinently, how long can a "nationalist" leader like Modi espouse the cause of Chinese business and allow China to use Gujarat to set up a manufacturing base to capture the Indian market?'

It is pertinent to note that the number of Chinese components that are used for 25 per cent of India's manufactured products, are projected to rise significantly over the next few years. This excessive dependence can be disrupted, if there is a strained relationship between the two countries. In such an event, to the detriment of India, supplies can be cut. This is an issue that is being discussed seriously in Indian diplomatic circles.

Even as he was trying to woo the Chinese in order to show US and UK that he was not solely dependent on them, Modi tried to soften Canada. Being close to the US, Canada was also very uncomfortable with the happenings in 2002 in Gujarat and had taken a strong view. But there is a large Gujarati expatriate community in Canada: the second largest Indian community in that country. The community has many associations to represent their cause: like the Canada Gujarat Construction Association and the Garvi Gujarat Association of Canada. Modi's men used such Gujarati bodies to lobby with the Canadian government to soften its stand. The fact that Canada too, is looking for investments and seeking to increase trade with India helped soften their stand,' admits a Canadian diplomat in India. He adds: 'It was a tussle between the human rights lobby, also represented strongly in the Canadian government, and the pro-business group and the latter won,' the diplomat said.

Swinging the deal for Modi indirectly was McCain Foods, the world's largest producer of French fries. The company – which rode into India by piggy-backing on McDonald's started contract farming for potatoes in Gujarat and set up a huge potato processing plant in the state's Mehsana district in 1997. That was before Modi's time.

'Obviously with a view to impress, the Modi government was very pro-active. Modi made available his private number and those of relevant officials to representatives of McCain Foods. The whole deal was done in a few days, faster than clearances take in Canada and this impressed McCain hugely,' the diplomat said.

Another Canadian company in Gujarat is Bombardier. The rail-passenger-coach manufacturing company has its manufacturing plant in Vadodara and the decision to invest was taken before Modi's time.

As a result of its growing presence in Gujarat, Canada became the partner-country at Vibrant Gujarat 2011. In the follow-up, many trade delegations from Gujarat have visited Canada and vice versa. Though these visits have not resulted in increased investments in Gujarat – except for McCain increasing the area under contract farming for potatoes – Canada was back for Vibrant Gujarat 2013 as the partner country once again.

Modi has been able to curry favour with Canada, even though his efforts to woo the US have not been successful as yet.

II

'Mahatma Modi': Building a Brand

After elections 2012 and with his prime ministerial campaign in full swing, Narendra Modi looked forward to 'Vibrant Gujarat 2013' as a great opportunity to further his cause. A star attraction at the show was to be a delegation from Pakistan. This was intentional: a Pakistani delegation at the Modi show would go a long way in enhancing his acceptability as an icon of development for Gujarat and therewith as well-qualified to lead India.

But as the saying goes: God disposes what man proposes. Two days before 'Vibrant Gujarat' began and following the brutal killing of two Indian jawans along the Line of Control (LoC), tensions between India and Pakistan escalated.

Predictably, the BJP upped the ante. Modi realized that presenting a Pakistani delegation at Vibrant Gujarat and conferencing with representatives of an 'enemy nation' would make him a butt of criticism.

Questions would be asked once again about Modi's stand on Sir Creek. Just before the trade fair and during electioneering, Modi had complained that Prime Minister Manmohan Singh was not doing enough to address the issue.

Accordingly, when the 10-member delegation from the Karachi Chamber of Commerce and Industry checked into a hotel at Ahmedabad, the Gujarat police advised them to 'keep away' from the Vibrant Gujarat show beginning in Gandhinagar the next day.

In fact, the group was requested to head back to Mumbai and leave India altogether.

When journalists asked the police about the Pakistani delegation, they said that the team had faced some problems with visas.

'They had visas only for Ahmedabad, not for Gandhinagar, where Vibrant Gujarat was being held', the police said.

The Pakistani delegation had come to Gujarat with specific interests in textiles, gems, and jewellery. Their visit had been planned after another by Pakistani representatives to a 'Chemical Expo' in Ahmedabad in 2012.

This team was in India for not just Vibrant Gujarat, they also wanted to visit Surat, which is home to a large number of diamond exporters. The earlier delegation to the 'Chemical Expo' had called on Modi, who had seemed open to the idea of cross-border trade. This had encouraged the Pakistanis to lobby Modi for a direct flight between Ahmedabad and Karachi.

A week before the Pakistani team to Vibrant Gujarat was forced to turn around, the Vishwa Hindu Parishad (VHP) had tried to bust the myth that it was development that enhanced Modi's acceptability for the post of prime minister.

VHP's mouthpiece, *Vishwa Hindu Samachar*, ran a cover story titled, 'What Gujarat does, India will have to do tomorrow.'

Hailing Narendra Modi's victory in the latest elections, the publication insisted that Modi had won on the plank of Hindutva, not development. It also commended Modi for not giving a single ticket to the Muslims and claimed that this was the reason why Hindus 'forgave' Modi for his earlier Sadbhavana mission (which was ostensibly an attempt to 'include' Muslims in the scheme of things).

'After the Sadbhavana mission, Modi realized that nothing but Hindutva could work in Gujarat: the Hindutva laboratory,' ran the article. It also pointed to how Modi had donned a saffron kurta in the advertising campaign for the Gujarat election to dispel any doubts that Hindus may have had.

The article quotes Modi during his campaign: '*Praja Ram Che, Hu Hanuman Chu*' (the people are my lords like Rama and I am their servant like Hanuman). He also revived the refrain of 'Ahmed Miyan,' (a reference to Ahmed Patel, the leader of the Congress, who, he said would become the chief minister of Gujarat if the Congress won the election). These tactics contributed considerably to Modi's victory.

'Elections cannot be won on the winds of development,' read the article. 'Atalji failed to return to power in 2004 on the Shining India campaign, Chandrababu Naidu also failed to get re-elected after focusing on development. Nano's fortunes were closely tracked all over the country. But then, why did BJP lose the Sanand seat in Nanotown (where the Nano factory is located)? If growth in the agricultural sector is 12 per cent per annum in Gujarat, why did Agriculture Minister Dilip Sanghani lose his seat in the last polls? Why did seven of Modi's ministers lose?'

Modi is, of course, very clear about how he won the elections. Immediately after the results were announced on 20 December, he blogged: 'This is a victory of developmental politics and good governance over everything else; it reflects a paradigm shift in electioneering in India. The results represent a comprehensive rejection of the partisan agenda of casteism, vote-bank politics, and divide and rule.' He added that under his rule, growth had been *sarvasparshi* (all-pervasive), *sarvasamneshak* (inclusive), and *sarvangi* (holistic).

The assertions of the VHP kick-started a lively debate in Gujarat. Although most analysts believed that Modi had won on the plank of development, VHP's contentions did get them thinking.

'The truth lies somewhere in between,' noted Harit Mehta, a journalist. 'Modi won partly for his agenda for development but also because many electors still viewed him as the icon of Hindutva.'

Modi's success has stemmed from maintaining a vote share of nearly 50 per cent in all the three elections that the BJP has fought under his leadership in Gujarat: 2002, 2007, and 2012. But everyone agrees that the win in 2002 – and again in 2007 – was solely due to his ability to consolidate Hindu votes.

'It was projected in the campaign that a win for Modi would take him to Delhi and make him a strong contender for the position of prime minister. This undoubtedly swung a lot of votes in his favour in Elections 2012. Otherwise, it was a mix of votes for Hindutva and development that helped him romp back to office,' says corporate consultant Sunil Parekh.

But the animated debate on Modi's victory in 2012 was not on the minds of corporate captains and foreign business representatives, when they gathered in Gandhinagar for the launch of Vibrant Gujarat on 11 January 2013.

Surprisingly, with the exception of Anil Ambani, most of the heads of industry were circumspect about endorsing Modi for prime ministership.

Ambani, on his part, compared Modi to Mahatma Gandhi and called the chief minister the 'king of kings'. 'Modi dreams with his eyes open. "Nara" in Sanskrit means Man and "Indra" is king,' Ambani added.

Other prominent industrialists, too, were fulsome in their praise of Modi, but none suggested his candidature for prime ministership.

Ratan Tata's successor at the Tata group, Cyrus Mistry, praised Modi for creating 'an enabling environment and infrastructure that helped attract investments.'

Adi Godrej of CII noted that it was Modi's futuristic approach that had made Gujarat one of the best investment destinations.

'Every state has followed Gujarat in holding investor summits. We look forward to the next five years under Mr Modi's leadership,' he said.

Essar's Shashi Ruia praised Modi's 'unparalleled' vision and said that the chief minister had demonstrated that good politics and good economics could co-exist.

Anand Mahindra called Gujarat 'the oasis of development' and conjectured how, in future, Gujarat's rate of growth could challenge that of China. 'A day will come in the not-too-distant future, when China will discuss and debate the Gujarat model of development like we debate the China model,' Mahindra said.

Announcing details of his proposed investments (Rs 100,000 crore) in Gujarat, Mukesh Ambani said that Reliance Industries was 'first a Gujarati company, then an Indian company and after that a global corporation.' He pointed out how Reliance had started from Gujarat, learned in the state and had now returned to the state to invest. Hailing 'Narendrabhai' as a leader with a grand vision and determination to translate this vision into reality, Mukesh Ambani said that Vibrant Gujarat was a celebration of that resolution to move forward. He disclosed that Reliance was investing in world-class institutions like the Deen Dayal Petroleum University in Gandhinagar, from where one day, 'Nobel laureates' would emerge.

Only Gautam Adani (of the Adani group and Modi's close associate) said that he hoped that 'Modi would migrate northwards' (read New Delhi).

The one other delegate who pushed Modi's case was neither a business baron nor an Indian. Konstanin Markelov, vice-governor of the tiny Astrakhan province of Russia, expressed the hope that Modi would win India's next general elections. Astrakhan had been Modi's first foreign destination after he became chief minister.

Sunil Mittal of the Bharti group, who, in 2009, had openly said that Modi would make a good prime minister, was missing at the show in 2013.

'Though many businessmen would love to see Modi as prime minister, they are wary of endorsing him publicly. Businessmen are by nature cautious. Having been chastened by Congress party representatives in 2009, many of them don't want to get into the bad books of the ruling Congress (at the Centre),' said Sunil Parekh, a corporate consultant now, but head of CII's Gujarat office earlier.

If Modi was disappointed by corporate captains not chanting 'Modi for PM', he did not show it. On the contrary, he projected an outward calm.

'We have proved that the branding of Gujarat has been better than that of any company in the world,' he said, inviting industrialists to return on 11 January 2015 for the next edition of Vibrant Gujarat.

By saying he would be there at the next edition of Vibrant Gujarat to receive them in person, Modi sparked off speculation about his own plans all over again.

Vibrant Gujarat 2013 saw delegations from 120 countries; during the two-day meet, there were 125 seminars, discussions and conferences.

Modi claimed that Vibrant Gujarat was a fascinating confluence of knowledge, thoughts and ideas from around the world for sustainable, holistic and inclusive development: terms which he had also used to describe his latest electoral victory. The Gujarat chief minister, who discarded the suit for traditional attire, said little about investment figures, preferring to concentrate on the 3.5 million jobs that would be created in Gujarat instead.

A total of 1200 companies displayed 25,000 products at the global trade show exhibition that was spread over a carpet area of 1 lakh square metres.

Subject to frequent criticism that Memorandums of Understanding (MoUs) signed at previous editions of Vibrant Gujarat had, so far, not translated into much on the ground, Modi's team restricted the number of investments proposed in 2013 to half of that at the last edition of the show. They also declared that Vibrant Gujarat was not only about attracting investments but primarily about forging partnerships.

An interesting feature of Vibrant Gujarat 2013 was that not every overseas participant sought to invest in Gujarat. Canada, which had a big team of 200 delegates including businessmen, diplomats, mayors, and other governmental representatives, was in desperate search of investments from Gujarati businessmen in their own country.

Canadian representatives extolled the great opportunities their country offered to Gujaratis in agriculture, natural gas, automobiles, education, clean energy, R&D, and life sciences. They also pointed to the large Gujarati business community that was already resident in Canada. Canada's minister for citizenship, immigration, and multiculturism, Jason Kenney said: 'We want to be part of the economic miracle called Gujarat.'

Almost like an answer to the Canadian prayer, Modi announced that the Gujarat State Fertilizer Corporation was to invest in a potash manufacturing facility in Canada. This would ensure domestic supply of potash fertilizer which was hitherto imported and therewith subject to the vagaries of international trade.

High-powered delegations from the US and UK were also present. The British business delegation was led by Patricia Hewitt, a former minister in Tony Blair's cabinet, while the 100-strong Japanese delegation was led by Japan's vice-minister for international affairs, Nabuhiko Sasaki. The Chinese presence at the show included a Chinese steel delegation and one from Yunan, led by Gao Shuxun, the province's vice-governor. Both the delegations had private meetings with Modi on the first day of the show.

The American delegation was led by the chief of the US-India business council, Ron Somers, who noted that Gujarat had seen 'stunning progress.' But given the large presence of Gujaratis in the US, organizations like the Asia-American Hotel Owners Association (AAHOA) were separately represented. Modi exhorted AAHOA to promote Gujarat in the US.

Analysts noted that such huge international delegations are not usually seen at conferences organized to showcase Indian business. Though the Modi government had sent delegations many months ahead of the show to lobby for, and ensure foreign participation, the fact that so many made the trip to the state is a clear indication that Gujarat is high up on the list of international investment destinations.

'Foreigners are bullish on Modi because they are convinced he is going to be India's next prime minister. On the other hand, Indian business groups, though backing Modi tacitly, still want to hedge their bets,' said an Indian employee of a western country's diplomatic mission in New Delhi.

Like the earlier editions of the show, Vibrant Gujarat 2013, too, showcased Gujarati culture on its sidelines. The show was tied up to Ahmedabad's annual kite festival, which coincides with Sankranti that is celebrated on 14 January every year. The more than 2000 foreign delegates at the show were treated to the sight of kites of various colours, sizes, and shapes flying over Ahmedabad. About 150 kite-flying enthusiasts from India, China, Italy, and Malaysia displayed their skills along the Sabarmati waterfront.

'The kites added colour to Vibrant Gujarat and were a befitting finale to the discourse on investment,' a journalist said.

'I read in the newspapers that Modi was received with adulation and much like a rockstar,' said RSS sympathizer Arvind Bosmia. 'Mukesh Ambani sat on the dais with Modi and other businessmen for three-and-a-half hours with their cell-phones dead'.

In the hall that could accommodate 5000 delegates, for 'security reasons', mobile signals had been jammed.

Such was the adulation, that whether Modi can garner votes or not, observers noted that he could surely be an effective fund-raiser for elections 2014.

Naturally, the Congress party was not very pleased at the huge corporate turnout at Vibrant Gujarat. This is clear from the remarks made by minister of state for information and broadcasting, Manish Tewari. When asked about the praise showered on Modi, Tewari pointed to Germany's era under a dictator.

'In the '30s, the German corporate sector held similar fascination for a gentleman who was at the helm of affairs there. The implications for the world at large were disastrous. I think corporate India should learn from history and draw appropriate lessons.'

Tewari also said that if there was any 'vibrancy' at all, it was in Maharashtra and that Tamil Nadu and Karnataka attracted more investment than Gujarat. 'They are just patting their own backs for nothing,' he remarked on Modi and his team.

Another Congress spokesman, Sandeep Dikshit, also tried to underplay the effusive praise for Modi, saying that it was not unusual for investors to praise the chief minister of a given state at such shows.

To Modi's fans, Tewari's statement is an indication that the Congress will go to any lengths to stem the rise of the Gujarat chief minister.

This belief gained strength with the appointment of a Lokayukta (public ombdusman) for Gujarat, who is seen as inimical to Modi. On 2 January 2013, less than a fortnight after Modi's latest electoral victory, the Supreme Court dismissed the objections filed by the Gujarat government and upheld the appointment of Justice R.A. Mehta as the Lokayukta of Gujarat. Indeed, coming barely ten days before Vibrant Gujarat, the announcement cast a shadow over the show aimed at attracting investment in the state.

'Now that they have appointed their own Lokayukta in Gujarat, they can institute cases against Modi,' speculated Arvind Bosmia. But how can cases be booked against a chief minister who is perceived as an honest man?

'False cases to harass him and damage his reputation can always be instituted. The Congress is known for this,' alleges Bosmia, betraying a trace of the nervousness that the appointment of the Lokayukta has unleashed in pro-Modi circles.

In August 2011, Justice Mehta had been appointed as the Lokayukta by the governor of Gujarat, Kamla Beniwal. At the time, the governor had consulted the chief justice of the Gujarat High Court on the appointment. While the Modi government too, received intimation, the governor did not seek its concurrence, ostensibly because the Gujarat government had left the position vacant for eight years and had shown no interest in filling it.

Seventy-eight-year-old Justice Mehta is a retired acting chief justice of the Gujarat High Court. He handles arbitration cases and also teaches law students. He is reputed to be very close to anti-corruption crusader Anna Hazare, who stayed in Justice Mehta's house the last time he was in Ahmedabad.

Given an objection filed by the Modi government, Justice Mehta had not yet taken up his new assignment as Lokayukta.

On the heels of the confirmation of Mehta as the ombudsman by the Supreme Court on 2 January, and therewith the overruling of the objection raised by the Gujarat government, triumphant Congress spokespersons in Delhi claimed that the Lokayukta would now reveal the truth behind corruption cases in Gujarat.

The fear unleashed by his new appointment may have to do with the innumerable indictments of the Gujarat government by the Comptroller & Auditor General (CAG) in its various reports about the functioning of the Gujarat government.

The CAG is mandated to not only examine and audit the annual performance of the central government and its various agencies, but also that of the state government and state government enterprises.

The last CAG report tabled on 31 March 2012 had highlighted irregularities worth ₹16707 crore by the Gujarat government.

A sizeable amount – ₹12400 crore – is attributed to operations of the Gujarat State Petroleum Corporation (GSPC) in the Krishna Godavari Basin, where funds to develop oil wells were overspent without producing any results.

CAG also pointed out that some undue benefits to some companies had resulted in losses to the exchequer.

At Vibrant Gujarat's previous chapters, the heads of many of these very companies had heaped praise on Modi's leadership.

For instance, it had been a company belonging to the Gautam Adani group, that had been the beneficiary of gas at below-par prices from the GSPC between 2006 and 2009. This deal had resulted in a loss of ₹70.5 crore to the exchequer.

Similarly, the GSPC had allowed Mukesh Ambani's Reliance Industry to install a platform in its block in KG Basin and had even agreed to maintain it.

Benefits worth ₹12 crore were also given to Essar Steel (run by Shashi Ruia) by the Gujarat State Petronet Corporation, which failed to recover the costs of the transport of gas supplied to the former.

Earlier CAG reports had pointed to the faulty management of various projects and the delays in their completion. It had also highlighted cases of undue benefits passed on to various contractors.

Modi's supporters now fear that the new ombudsman, Justice Mehta, could pick up from where these CAG reports left off, to further probe irregularities.

'No government is absolutely corruption free – not even the Modi government. But this should not be used as a stick by the Congress government-appointed Lokayukta, to harass Modi at a time when his star is on the ascendant. This would be unfair,' said a BJP politician.

Index